A Mother's Heart

Edited by: Dr. Cassundra White-Elliott

Cover picture: The cover picture represents five generations of mothers (one is a mother-to-be and one is a future mother).

In the upper left corner is Mildred M. (Dunlap) Williams. She was the matriarch of the Williams' family. She was the mother of ten children, one of whom was Gloria L. (Williams) Harrison, (upper right corner). Mildred was the grandmother to seventeen grandchildren, one of whom is Dr. Cassundra White-Elliott (bottom left). Both Mildred and Gloria are now deceased.

Gloria was the mother of four children, one of whom is Dr. Cassundra White-Elliott and the grandmother of eight, one of whom is Quantanique S. Williams (bottom right).

Quantanique is Dr. C's niece and Mildred's great-granddaughter.

The little girl is Kimara T'sehai Faith White. She is Dr. C's granddaughter, Gloria's great-granddaughter, Mildred's great-great-granddaughter, and Quantanique's second cousin.

Published by CLF Publishing, LLC. 3281 Guasti Road, Seventh Floor, Ontario, CA 91761. (760) 669-8149.

Copyright © 2013 by Cassundra White-Elliott. All rights reserved. No portion of this book may be reproduced, stored in a retrieval system, or transmitted by any form or any means electronically, photocopied, recorded, or any other except for brief quotations in printed reviews, without the prior permission of the publisher.

Cover Design by Senir Design. Contact information- info@senirdesign.com.

ISBN # 978-0-9892358-0-8

Printed in the United States of America.

Dedications

This book is dedicated to mothers around the world with a special dedication to my mother Gloria L. Harrison, who departed this life March 7, 2010 and to my friend Keisha Williams, who departed this life in May 2012.

Keisha Williams

A note from Keisha's son, Nathaniel Williams, Jr.

Life with my mother had its ups and downs, but I loved my mother and told her everything that had to do with my life. I was her first born, and we were the best of friends, even with all the whoopings I got. She taught me how to drive and how to treat a lady. I always went to her about my woman problems. Although my mom was nice and kind, she was protective over my baby sister and me. Despite the fact that she's no longer here, she is still here in a way because her rules and knowledge are left behind.

My mother was a saved holy person. At night while everyone was asleep, she would walk around the house praying and rubbing anointed oil on our foreheads and every door, so that unknown or unwanted spirits could not come and disrupt our family. She was a well-respected lady and never judged anyone without reason and tolerated a lot. Saying that our family misses our loved one and wishes the outcome would have been different is an understatement. But as life goes on, we continue to remember and love her as if she were still in our lives today.

Acknowledgements

I appreciate each of the twenty contributors to this book. Each chapter was written with love and respect for a wonderful woman. I thank each of you for your willingness to participate in this book and your adherence to all requests. This book is a success because of you!

Table of Contents

Introduction — 7

Blessed All Your Life by Isaac Thompson — 11
The Stella Thompson Story

The Love of Two Sons by Nicholas and Justin Harrison — 19
The Shonda Harrison Story

Love Never Lost by Ashleigh Morris — 31
The Cressie Daniels-Marshall Story

My Mother, God's Friend by Jerry G. Martin — 43
The Ormie B. Martin Story

The One I Adore by La'Charee Robinson — 51
The Mary Robinson Story

Ups and Down, but Together… by Eyounae Hayes — 65
The Maisha D. Hartfield Story

Unconditional Love by Jourdan Jovel — 75
The Franzette Kyles Story

An Irreplaceable Bond by Khalil Flemister — 81
The Eyana Flemister Story

Forgiveness by Audrey Albrecht — 89
The Francine Duff Story

The Strength of One Woman by Cathy Vines-Nichols — 97
The Mary Ann Vines Story

Mommy and Me by Akayla Clayton — 105
The Wanda Clayton Story

Through it All, I'm Still Standing by Dalejuan Jackson — 113
The Diane Jackson Story

Mommy by Quantanique Williams — 123
The Esperanza Green Story

The Love I Have for My Mother by Millicent Redd — 127
The Vertie Mae McClinton Story

A Mother Like None Other by Ayleeyah Nichols — 133

The Mercer Yvonne McClinton Story

Mom- Gentle Strength by Julia Lary   145
The Mildred Mae Williams Story

A Mother's Love by Tundra Alfred   157
The Katherine Heath Story

My Mom by Micaiah Alfred   167
The Tundra Alfred Story

A Mother's Undying Love by Dr. C. White-Elliott   173
The Gloria L. Harrison Story

A Mother's Love Shines, even During by Daron White   187
The Dr. Cassundra White-Elliott Story

The Gift of Salvation for Non-Believers   193

About the Editor   201

Other Books by the Editor   203

Introduction

Mothers around the world have dedicated their lives to their children. They take seriously the task of nurturing, loving, developing, educating, and preparing them for life. However, unbeknownst to most mothers, they face a task that is embedded with many challenges, such as the life of a teenager, rebellion, the terrible two's, etc. Despite the challenges, mothers forge ahead with the task at hand. With the love they have for their children, they endure many hardships, even when the same love is not returned or fully appreciated. They strive to stay focused on the task at hand and refrain from allowing anything to deter them.

On this road of motherhood, women embark upon this journey without a manual. They enter motherhood not fully knowing what to expect from the children they will raise. They don't know what the children's behavior patterns will be, their likes or dislikes, or how they will respond to different life experiences. Motherhood is truly on-the-job training.

Through the joys and pains, through the tears and metaphorical rain, mothers press on. At times, their love is equally reciprocated while at other times it is not. At times, children are found to be treasures, and at other times, they are not. At times, children are found to be obedient, while at other times, they are not. One constant you will find is – regardless of how the children are, mothers would not trade their children in for anything else in the world. Mothers take their children as they are!

Because of this unconditional love, their endurance, and their commitment, mothers are worth their just due. They are worthy of praise, and they are worthy of honor.

In this book, you will read the stories of many mothers written by their children who wanted to honor them. Some of the mothers have passed on, but their memories remain. The other mothers who are being honored are alive and well. They will have the opportunity to read the words their children have written.

Please note- this book is not to paint mothers as saints. It is to show their humanness, their successes and their mistakes, their triumphs and their trials. It is to honor them for all they have done. By no means are mothers perfect, but with their love, they have seen their children through many battles. It is because of who they are/were that we are who we are.

After examining the lives of my grandmother, mother and aunts and being a mother and grandmother myself, I know the sacrifices a mother makes for her children. A mother always wants what is best for her children. She will give them the dress from her back and the food from her plate to make sure her children are well cared for.

As you read through the story of each mother, I want you to think about a mother you know. She may be your mother, your grandmother, your aunt, a friend, a cousin, a sister, a mother-in-law, or a co-worker. As you think about this mother, think about how you can encourage her. Whether you know it or not, mothers need to be encouraged. They need to know that their labor is not in vain.

When my mother was alive, I told her, "Thank you for loving me. Thank you for teaching me. Thank you for placing me above all else. Thank you for being my mother."

Today, I encourage the young mothers in my life. I tell them when they are doing a great job with their children, especially the mother of my grandchildren. Also, I give them pointers (in love) when they can do better. I believe my words encourage them to be tender, loving mothers. As I speak to the young mothers, I must remember that they are relatively new to mothering, and they are learning through the joys and challenges of motherhood, just as I did when raising my two sons.

To all mothers- we cannot change the past. We cannot undo any mistakes we may have made. All we can do is strive for a better tomorrow for ourselves and for our children. Be encouraged! You are not alone in this job of motherhood. There are many mothers who share your concerns, your worries, and your fears.

Motherhood is a joy. Enjoy every moment of your adventure and spend as much time with your children that you can. Love them with all heart, and whether you experience ups and downs or a smooth ride, your children will never forget your love.

Dr. Cassundra White-Elliott

Blessed All Your Life

The Stella Thompson Story
by
Isaac Thompson

Stella and Isaac

A Mother's Heart

One's appreciation of long life and the numbering of your days by God takes on a special aura when memories are encased in love. Maybe it's because I reside in a place where movies are made, that early recollections cast Mom as the first glamorous vision of my mind's eye. In those long ago days, there were restaurants with long counters for those whose preference was counter service. So when I saw Mother at work behind the counter in a uniform, all put-together to deal with the public, so stylish that repeat customers were a certainty, the vision was like those women on television. As a tiny kid, I remember the smile that made me feel special and the beverage she gave me in that restaurant-type tall thick glass. Since she too was young, her figure was thin and curvy, just like the actresses on T.V.

The past few decades gave rise to the term latch-key kids. I guess as a society, we're prone to developing terms descriptive of an individual or a family's composition or circumstances. For minorities, it seems that households with two working parents have been the norm since seemingly forever.

It had been the time of year when fall was giving way to winter, and I found myself sitting on the stoop of our Long Island home, waiting for Dad, when dropping temperatures led to a decision (perhaps resulting in automatic discipline) from some inner place.

I decided it was too cold to merely wait, so going to the rear of our home, I broke a small basement window, because well, I was cold. The results were anything but unpleasant; rather, the next day, Mom gave me my own house key! Being all of seven years old, I realized Mother believed in me as a person. Of course, the responsibility came with a list of do's and a "don't lose it" (and a requisite safety pin "so I wouldn't lose it"). Raising responsible children requires trust, a belief that the parents' words will be heeded, and they were.

A life-long aspect of character grew from the latch-key norm of those times. That element was a work ethic, established as the norm, from the earliest memory of Mom and Dad, but an unspoken life example delivered simply by observation. Even without the privileges I've enjoyed, due to higher education benefits, Mom always found a way to earn more, keeping up with established professional positions. The restaurant work gave way to nursing and licensed health care, establishing an equal footing in the mother/father dynamic.

Comfortable living and upwardly mobile households bring expectations. For Mom's three boys, it meant doing well in school; after all, we had no excuses. When love is combined with good-provision, it's up to the children to make their parents proud. Since Dad was former military, he was not given to heaping praise; it was simply his way to expect one to do as expected.

So it was Mother, the one that would occasionally praise, who would cause my chest to proudly swell. Then, came the lesson; comportment, behavior carried as much weight as doing one's best in any subject. I can only recall it as pre-high school and the dreaded report card day. Well, there I was head high and confident. Good grades, yeah, with one glaring exception: the red-letter in citizenship. Having become socially self-assured, I'd been too talkative. When the evening of reckoning arrived, all the other grades didn't matter. I'd blown it by talking too much! Stern words left me feeling small, level with the carpet, unable even to offset the single issue by pointing out academic achievement. A lifelong lesson was never lost. Sure, Dad was Dad, but when your mother is not happy, the whole house feels it. Thank God! When you're raised with standards originating from God-Almighty, well, it establishes an expectancy of being all you can be- period. Character and behavior, I later learned, had been ingrained by my mom's dad, and no son of hers would be exempt from carrying the mantle of God-fearing, God-obeying, Christian folk. Uh, I think the lesson took!!!

As often happens, love is extended from mother to son in ways neither could foresee as being life shaping. An otherwise normal Saturday morning has become a lifelong blessing. Strange, how the memory of a day five decades ago remains so vivid. Mom instructed this middle son in the basics of cooking. It was not just the cooking; the fare was common-place food: bacon, grits and eggs. What was not common was wisdom's foresight, her realizing that no matter the twists and turns of life, a man should be able to take care of himself in all aspects. In light of that awareness, not only was I schooled in self-preservation, but also in things from food to healthy living, housekeeping and other things too numerous to recall that provided life lessons designed for self-sufficiency.

We don't always realize at the time, but our care and instruction for one child has generational reverberations. During my times as a single dad, occasionally my job would require travel. The proximity of my parent's home meant minimal disruption for my son, although at the time that provided small comfort in easing the guilt of being away from home. It was not until years later that I learned my folks were somewhat put off by the in-depth instructions I would leave. You see the guilt was two-fold, not wanting to impose on Mom whose job had been done was the second aspect. But with written instructions, lunch menus, pre-ironed clothes and on and on, I did not take into account, they'd **raised me**! So what took place and is still resounding generationally is love, abiding in all things. Having seen it looking back, witnessing it in the here and now, and reveling in what's to come, leaves a son with an all too insufficient "Thanks, Mom."

Life's journey, the one we share, carries some pain and losses (husband-dad, son-brother and so forth) and is, as with life itself, peppered with highs and lows. A low water mark came on Father's Day 1993, when settling in and basking in the one day a good dad can feel good through the outpouring of love in its purest that darn phone rang. The message was inconceivable. Mom's life was jeopardized by a car accident while traveling. So horrible was the thought that I hoped it was a cruel prank. It was not.

While details are too numerous and varied, my mother emerged from a near comatose state three days later and subsequently was stabilized enough for us to return and have her surgery, involving metal-plates, screws, etc., overseen by our family doctor. The depth of despair I cannot fully convey, but it was my first intense petition to the Rock, our Savior Jesus, to spare my mother; and the only time I ever uttered "take me instead," reasoning that my son has for himself a mom second to none. Interspersed during the time of waiting for Mom's vital signs to be restored were days spent alone in Bakersfield motel room, fielding phone calls at all hours, from Hawaii to Florida. Over and over, I'd hear, "Well, I'm glad you're with her," which really made me want to scream!

When one feels helpless and despair takes him somewhere he has never been, only our Lord can gird His own to do what they're called to do. That accident changed my mother's life, requiring special consideration at x-ray machines, etc., but it also changed my life, as I still have a most difficult time dealing with Father's Day of '93.

"How do you thank the one," is a portion of the songwriter's words for those whose caretaking is beyond description. Well, perhaps, believers can grasp that of all else, **a legacy of faith**, of being a **people of God** is the single most important thing we give to those whose lives our Father entrusted to our care. When it comes to my mom, I know God loves me by whom and through whom He gave me life. Since our human journey carries necessary struggles, designed for our eternal well being, no matter, come what may, this mother's son can always recall her singular declarative view of her second born: "You've been blessed all your life." Yes Mother, I have, and it all began with you.

Praise be to God

The Love of Two Sons for Their Mother

The Shonda Evans-Harrison Story
by
Nicholas and Justin Harrison

The Harrison Family: Shonda, Justin, Nicholas, and August

A Mother's Heart

Nicholas' Testimony

Someone to shelter and guide us, to love us, whatever we do, with a warm understanding and infinite patience, to watch over her children and treasure them all through the years, a mother, that is.

My existence has been momentously influenced by my mother, Shonda Evans-Harrison. Responsive, nurturing, genuine, and protective would best describe my mother's merits. She is one of the few individuals who have aided me through hectic circumstances. She is my go-to person. If something happened to me or if I needed someone to talk to, she would be the first I turn to. And though I turn to her often and constantly with some form of request, she never turns me away. She was able to answer every question I had, to the best of her knowledge. The majority of the times we communicated, I did not comprehend what she meant, and she recognized my confusion.

I believe admiration is a form of respect. I admire my mother just as much as she admires me. I admire how fair-minded she is. She does not favor anyone over another. She treats people evenly.

Because I am the eldest, I was taught that I will be held responsible for my brother and the rest of the family if something happens to my parents. I admit I was afraid once she told this to me. But, I knew exactly what she meant during the process of growing up. My understanding of my mother's viewpoint helped me become a healthier, responsible individual. She had also taught me to be myself and have positive people surround me. She convinced me to believe that being different was something special to be proud of. Being yourself leads to a better lifestyle. This is how I became well-rounded and social. My mother knows what is best for me and my brother. She motivates us to be prepared to make the right choices.

I knew when something bothered her, and I understood when it was necessary to give her space, but I also knew how to comfort her when no one was available. The relationship between my mother and me is indefinable. We were able to help each other, which was odd for me to realize that I could be there for someone who is always supportive.

I have witnessed the traumatic times my mother had struggled to further her education, raise a family, and find employment. As independent as she was, her actions and choices always resulted in an optimistic outcome. There was something about her that I yearned for. I grew up thinking she had superpowers to make her solve problems efficiently. The reason for this was because she was also raised that way by her parents.

Ever since my maternal grandmother passed away, the qualities I saw in my mother dropped. It was a dreadful period. My mother became weak and hopeless for a long time. This frightened me so much that I did not know what to do. Days were spent in her room, reminiscing about her life through old photographs and letters. This was an unforgettable experience that helped me shape my outlook on life.

My mother was living in silence and was complex about her situations. Because I was scared at first, my mind changed from fearing her to sympathizing with her. I realized from her eyes, she had a durable resistance to illness and a strong will to live an ordinary life under such terrible circumstances. Giving my small gifts, I also received from her a more valuable gift- true happiness. True happiness comes from the simple things in life and from trying to make others happy. The more of it we give to others, the more we will have for ourselves.

What I love most about my mother is how she is capable of making things and life easy when it isn't. A while before I came into existence, my mother had become saved. She taught my brother and me about the Lord. She kept the Bible as a guide to raising us. In turn, we all got saved, and the Lord has continued to be the guide in our lives even when we were not around her.

My mother has proven that the qualities of determination and perseverance are both essential to have in order to undertake our mindsets. She has lectured my brother and me on the fundamental values of life necessary to survive in this world. By doing so, we have extensive conversations about her experiences, memories and accomplishments. I look forward to utilize my mother's attributes for future situations.

My mother is actually an ordinary woman, but in her tiny appearance lays an extraordinary fortitude, perseverance, an altruistic soul, and a very kind heart. The kind of mother who brought me up with her whole kindly heart, the kind of persistent woman with strong willpower who had to face the toughest challenges in life, and the kind of person who always demonstrated great eagerness for every tragic lives without requiring anything in return and great willingness to help everyone's misery though she did not have much. My mother taught me more than anyone else, not only inspired in me the strength to overcome hardships in my life, but also left me with invaluable life lessons. Her fortitude and perseverance, as well as her kind heart, have encouraged me to grow up to live the life of an authentic person, a life engulfed with perseverance and determination, a life with heartfelt eagerness to love and to receive love from every one and optimistic beliefs in the future.

I am highly thankful of the awareness to appreciate our mothers on a designated day. Nevertheless, mothers ought to receive the praise they deserve for all of their hard work and effort. Because I am a child by heart, regardless of age, I will continue to call her "mommy." It does not bother her whenever I say this. She mentions that I will always be her baby no matter how old I am. I love her so much, and I appreciate everything she has done.

Suffering through her absence for a number of years (due to her hospitalization), my family and I are able to continue functioning the way my mother would want us to. She always told me that I should be alright and know what to do if she is not here. This is a challenge I am prepared to face. It has been a fearsome roller coaster. Lamentably, numerous events took place without her support. Birthdays, school events, and family get-togethers have not been the same without her. I miss her dearly. I feel miserable hearing other people bring up their mothers and how much fun they have with them.

I look to her in hopes that someday I will be as content, as resilient, and as coherent as she. She has taught me the most important thing in life- never give up on yourself. I thank her dearly for aiding me to become who I am today. I would have never made it as far as I have without her comfort. The precious lessons from my mother are the luggage for me to go on my road and discover new horizons of knowledge and make my dream become a reality instead of just a dream. I owe my strength to my mother. Her life experience has made me more vigorous to face every hardship, to overcome each failure, and move on. Far more meaningfully, I also realize the invaluable gift of life and true happiness to view the world more optimistically and to believe in a brighter future.

Justin's Testimony

My mother has been an inspiration to me since the day I was born. I learned to love my mom since we first met, and I will always love her. She always protects me and supports me through thick and thin. Whenever I am happy or whenever I am sad, my mother is with me. She helps me with hard problems in life and is glad for some of the choices I've made.

From raising me to teaching me life lessons, my mother has always been there for me from the start. My mother has raised me to be a great man in life. The way I act is no differently than the way any other person should. I was raised with respect, manners, my own dignity, and to have my own self confidence. Every day, I see kids and how they act around each other. Then, I think to myself, *I'm glad I was raised properly by a mother who cares.*

One of the lessons my mother taught me was to treat everyone I know with respect. She has treated me with respect, the majority of the time, to help me learn. I had even asked her, "What if I treat someone with respect, but he doesn't choose to respect me the same way?" That's when she told me it does not matter if people treat me terribly. As long as I know how to treat people properly, with the right amount of respect, I will have respect for myself.

Ever since I learned that from her, I have treated most people with respect. And I honestly do not care what others say or think about me. I have also learned from my mother that I can succeed at anything I work hard at. She always wants me to succeed in school, so I can have a good education and go to college when I get older. She also wants me to succeed in following my dream of becoming a doctor. I have wanted to become a doctor because of my mom. I learned all about doctors and how to become one from her.

I love how my mother and I look alike. In similarities, we have the same eyes, nose, smile, and most importantly, the same personality. I would always say what my mother would say, eat what my mother would eat, and also act the same way she did. She always called me her little twin. And her friends and our family would call me "Little Shonda." Hearing that from others would always make me smile, and it would make me happy inside.

What I didn't understand about my mother is that she sometimes kept her feelings inside. I had even told her that it's not healthy to ball up all of your feelings and not tell anyone about it. I was afraid that my mother would become insanely stressed with everything around her. If something terrible had happened, or if she were to be upset, she would just hold all of her feelings inside, until she would be able to let it out. If my mother was going through a hard time with work or family, she would take her anger out on my brother, my father, and me. But I understood what she was going through.

Sometimes I felt that if I bothered my mom while she was upset, I would get yelled at and make her even more upset than she already was. Little did I know that every now and then, my mother actually needed for me to come bother her and talk to her. Every day when my mom would come home from work, I would ask her, "How was your day, Mom?" She would then smile and tell me how her day went. Even if she was stressed, me asking her that question would please her.

My mother would always sit down with me and tell me why she was upset and what her problems were. After our little talks, she would thank me for taking the time to sit and listen to her and help her solve her problems. Seeing my mother happy made me happy. I knew that when she was happy, nothing would ever change.

Whenever my mom would be in a good mood, she would always call me her "Jiglet." She started calling me that when I was born; I never knew what that meant and was never told how she came up with that word. But it didn't matter, because my mother loved calling me that name, and she loved me as well. Knowing that my mother loved me meant everything to me. I love my mom with all my heart. And she had once told me, "Whenever I yell or scream at you, I'm simply doing that because I love you."

From there on, I never really cared if my mother would yell at me or get upset with me. Because I knew that she loved me no matter what. The one thing that I admire about my mother is how she always cares about others. She is kind, incredibly friendly, loving, and so warm hearted. Not only would she care, but she would take care of the ones she loved. From taking care of me and my brother, to taking care of other family members, my mother was there for everyone. She would try her best to please everyone.

My mother is an independent, strong, smart, confident woman. I am grateful to have a mom that takes care of me. I know that I can always rely on my mother for help, advice, and all sorts of lessons she can teach me. When I struggle to bring myself to happiness, my mother is there to help me. Never have I taken anything that my mother has done for me for granted. My mother cooks for me, cleans for me, buys me clothes, she keeps a house over my head, and keeps me safe.

I believe that my mother, Shonda Evans-Harrison, is the greatest mother that myself or anyone else can have. She gave birth to me and my older brother Nicholas. I'm proud to be called her son. I would not be able to enjoy the rest of my life without my mother in it. I am who I am today because of my wonderful mother. I would not be here today if it weren't for my mother.

I honestly care about my mom, and I wouldn't want anything unfortunate to happen to her. She is everything I could ever ask for in a mother. The most important thing I love about my mother is that no matter how many times we fight, no matter how many times we argue, even if I am not the best child she could ever have, she always makes me feel that I am the best gift she ever received from God.

Looking back at the wonderful times I had with my mother, I remember she is the most positive and important influence in my life. She is a diligent and determined woman who has left me with the right direction in life. But more importantly, she has helped me appreciate this life she has given me with happiness.

Love Never Lost

The Cressie Latrice Daniels-Marshall Story
by
Ashleigh Morris

Cressie and daughters: Ashleigh and Kyleigh

A Mother's Heart

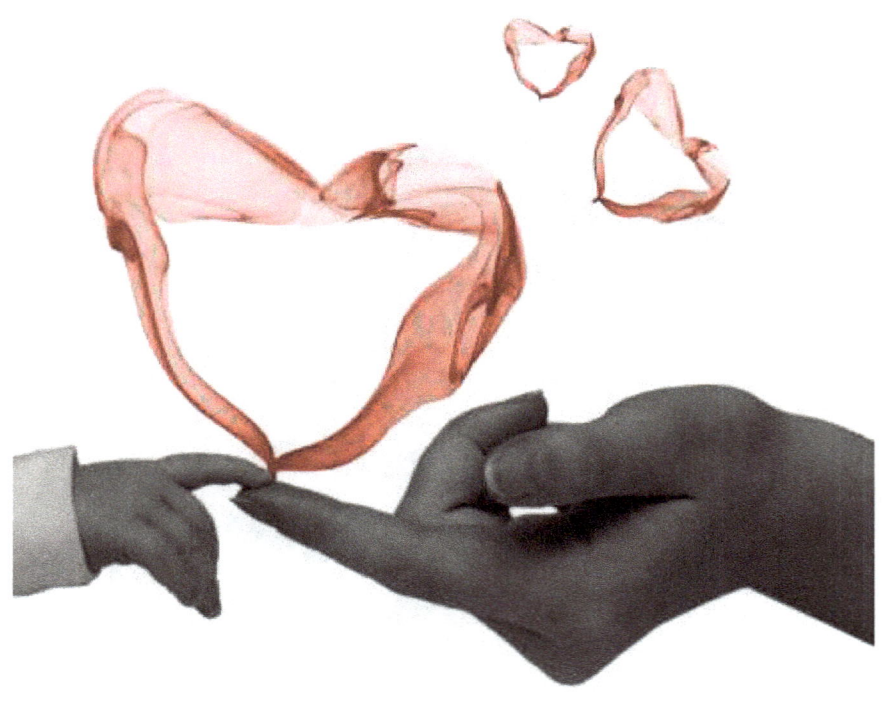

It wasn't always perfect, nor was it always bad. We all have a time in our lives where things just don't go our way or how we had imagined they would.

Growing up, I had a great life. I didn't want for anything. I got everything I wanted and more, and my life couldn't be any better. No, I didn't grow up with both parents in the home, but I had both parents in my life. I was my mother's only child up until three months before my seventh birthday. I didn't want a sister or a brother, but I had no choice in that.

The following year in August of 1998, I experienced my first heart break. I lost my grandmother to cervical cancer at the age of 47 years old. I was only seven, so I didn't know what my mom was going through, nor did I give it much thought. Life went on, and I still had a great life even having a little sister. We took mini family trips, and we were always together with my uncle's family.

Fast forwarding to about 2002, my mom had the gastric bypass surgery, and I believe that's when everything changed. Once she lost the weight, she started going out and being around different crowds of people.

In 2005, I began to notice her constant drinking. I'm not sure how long it had been going on, but that is when I opened my eyes. That same year, I moved with my dad for my sophomore year of high school, only to move back with my mom the following year as I had to be a protector for my sister, who had seen and been around too much for my liking. People are different when they are drunk.

Unfortunately for me, my mother was not the happy type of drunk. She would get drunk and angry, and she would become a person whom I did not know. People would call her by the name Mello, and I feel that was an alter ego. To this day, I can't stand for a person to call her Mello. The mother I knew and loved was Cressie. This Mello person that she turned into when she drank, I often felt, did not love me. I expressed how I felt to my mom a few times once she was sober, and she would apologize and let me know how much she does in fact love me.

There was a program in my apartment building, and they would set the kids up on summer jobs for three weeks, and they would get paid $300 at the end of the three weeks. I was planning to go shopping at the outlets, so I gave my money to my mom to hold until I was going. The day before I was set to go, I got in trouble for something, but she still let me go. However, she told me she would not be giving me my money that I had worked for. Imagine that!

Summer 2007 was when my life hit rock bottom. Don't get me wrong. I was a child that got whoopings and punishments. So even though I had a good life, if I did the crime, I paid the time. It seems though the older I became, the harsher she became, even when I hadn't done anything to deserve it.

When I was sixteen, I was going to summer school and working my first job at Knott's Berry Farm. My school was on the same street as my job, so I didn't mind catching the bus, but when I got off at midnight, my ride should have been there. Right? Wrong!!

There were a few times I had to wake people up out of their sleep to come and pick me up because my mom was out at the club and forgot she was supposed to pick me up from work. How she managed to forget about her sixteen year old getting off work at 12am is beyond me, but hey what could I do?

The day I will never forget is December 22, 2007. My hardheaded sister and I were 'play' fighting. I told her over and over again to stop because I did not want to play around with her anymore. I was not supposed to hit my sister, but I had continually told her to leave me alone. When I did hit her, it sounded louder than it really was and she became dramatic. My mom started yelling at me and told me, "You're almost 300 pounds. You shouldn't be hitting on her."

By that time, I was in my room, so in my defense I yelled out to her, "I'm not close to 300 pounds!" She ran into my room, and she called me every name in the book. By that time, I was called a b**** and fat, and she said wished she had an abortion with me, and more. I was in tears at the words that were coming out of her mouth and the reason why it all started. She grabbed a bottle of baby lotion off my dresser and threatened to throw it at my face, so I asked her, "What are you doing? Why are you doing this?" She then had the bottle in the air to throw it, so I tried to grab it.

I should have just let her throw it at my face because she then swore that my almost 300 pound self was trying to fight her, so she ran into her room and grabbed an aluminum bat. She came back and hit me on my leg with it. It wasn't a tap; she swung and hit me. I then grabbed my phone and ran out the house with no shoes on. She grabbed my hair and told me to give her her phone. I was still trying to get away with the phone because I needed to call my dad to come get me. I had no choice but to give her the phone because my head was starting to hurt.

Once she let go, I turned around and told her I hated her. Of course, I did not mean it, but at the time I wanted her to feel the same pain that I felt. I went to a neighbor's house that's like an aunt to me and took my ponytail down. All of the braids on my left side fell to the floor. To this day, the hair doesn't grow right there.

That was it. If it had not been my senior year, I would have transferred schools and left then and there. Was this really how my winter break was starting? She called the neighbor's house the next day wanting to talk to me, but I had already gone to my grandmother's house to get my dad's number, and he was coming that night. I went to pack my clothes, and she was saying how sorry she was. Of course, I forgave her. She gave me my phone, I got my things, and I left.

February rolled around, and it was time to take my senior pictures. At the last minute, she told me she didn't want to take me because I had started getting my dress made without her the weekend before. But, she had not wanted to take me, so a friend ended up taking me. So the day of my pictures, I was dressed and ready to go. I was in tears because I had an appointment at the place. I didn't need her money. I just needed her to take me, but she wasn't budging. I walked over to another neighbor's house, who is also considered like an aunt to me, and she wiped my tears, fixed my hair because I had been sweating, and took me.

On the Thursday night before my prom, I do not remember what the disagreement was over, but again I was out of the house and at the same aunt's house who took me to take my pictures. This time I managed to take my phone. She was telling my aunt she wasn't giving me my prom dress or clothes for school the following morning. I cried myself to sleep. The next day at school, I got a call to go to the office, and I saw my cousin walking to the office as well. I went in and my mom was standing in the front to pick us up. I was so scared because I thought she was going to kidnap us or something. I got a text from my aunt saying she had to pick things up for my champagne party, and my mom was picking us up, and she was meeting us at the nail shop. We left, and my mother never mentioned anything from the previous night.

The day before I graduated, it was bad. I had all my things packed and was ready to go. My sister and I had agreed that we would both be leaving this time, but she was leaving after summer, and I was leaving after I walked the stage. I moved the morning after grad night.

So 2008 was when I moved with my dad. I went to visit frequently, and we talked all the time. We came to the realization that our relationship works better when we are not living under the same roof. There were times I visited and said I would never go back, but I couldn't stay away too long. She was always apologizing for what we had been through. I was still hurting from that because I wondered how could this person whom I love more than anyone else in this world do these things and say these things to me.

In 2010, I had to move back. I thought my life was over. I had to apply for the county and was getting $200 dollars a month and food stamps. I never in my life wanted to do that. But like people told me, it's okay if you use it as the assistance that it is. I moved back in March and started working for the post office in October and got myself off the county assistance. Things were good until she wanted me to pay so much money for things that I was always broke, even with a job.

Then the arguing started again, and I couldn't take it, so a year after I moved back, my boyfriend and I got an apartment. She was angry at first, but she got over it, and our relationship was the relationship I had always wanted from her. 2011 was the start of great things with me and her. We hung out. She would come over my house, and I would go over hers. We talked on the phone every single day. I just loved her so much, and I was finally starting to feel the love I always longed for. We still argued, but we were so much alike that it had to happen. We never fought like we did before though. We were both stubborn with bad attitudes.

We brought in the 2012 New Year together, and a few days later, I was taking her to the hospital. The lining of her stomach was gone, and the doctors blamed it on the drinking. She had stopped drinking hard liquor and was only drinking wine. When this happened, she stopped completely because she needed to be here for her girls.

In April, she was back at the hospital, and this time they say it was a mass that didn't need to be removed because it had shrunk in the time she was there. I was enjoying my mother. There was not a day I went without talking to her. I invited her to my coworker's church for Mother's Day, and we joined the Sunday after.

My mother hadn't been to church in over five years. But then, every Sunday, my mom, my sister, and I would be at church. She wouldn't always feel good before services, but she didn't miss.

On September 10, 2012, I got the call that would change my life forever. My mom had been in the hospital over the weekend, and they were running tests. She called to tell me she had stomach cancer. I was at a loss for words. I went to my job and told them I would need the week off. I was at that hospital with her every day. The following week, they transferred her to a different hospital, and when she arrived, she told me her cancer was at Stage 4. That was the first and last time my mom saw me cry over her illness.

Though I knew how serious it was, I didn't imagine her drying. I knew we would fight this, and everything would be okay. She was at my birthday celebration October 9th. She got married October 20th. Everything was perfect. I was taking her to her chemo every other Tuesday. I didn't mind doing anything for her. One time though, we had an argument, so I missed a week of seeing her. I told her, "I think I'm crowding you, and I need to give you space because I am coming over every chance I get and calling so much."

When I went and I saw her for the first time in over a week, I couldn't believe my eyes. I stood at the door with tears in my eyes. Her face was so sunken in, and she was so small. She had been losing so much weight, and I had been seeing her so much that I was the only person who didn't notice. Then her husband was getting her dressed and bathing her, and my sister was putting her legs on and off the couch for her. It was crazy to me. This independent woman had to depend so much on people. I hated it for her.

On November 18, 2012, she asked me to take her to emergency to get a breathing treatment. I had no clue it would be the last time she rode in my car or asked me to take her somewhere. My mother Cressie Latrice Daniels-Marshall died November 20, 2012. She was still apologizing to me about our relationship until her last breath. I had forgiven her, and I didn't care about that anymore. I just didn't want her to leave me.

She was that one person that no matter what I could call and depend on for anything. She was that one person who was going to always be there. She was that one person who made sure I was always okay. But now that one person is gone. And she left me with a huge responsibility: looking after not only myself but my fifteen-year-old sister. My sister and I have gotten closer; we now have a bond that is unbreakable.

It is hard not having my mother, and this heartache can be unbearable, but I rather her be in heaven pain free than on this earth living in the pain she was in that no one knows about but her. All that we went through only made us stronger and made me the woman that I am. I wouldn't take anything back because the relationship we had in the end was perfect!!

My Mother, God's Friend

The Ormie B. Martin Story
by
Jerry G. Martin

Ormie and Her Children

A Mother's Heart

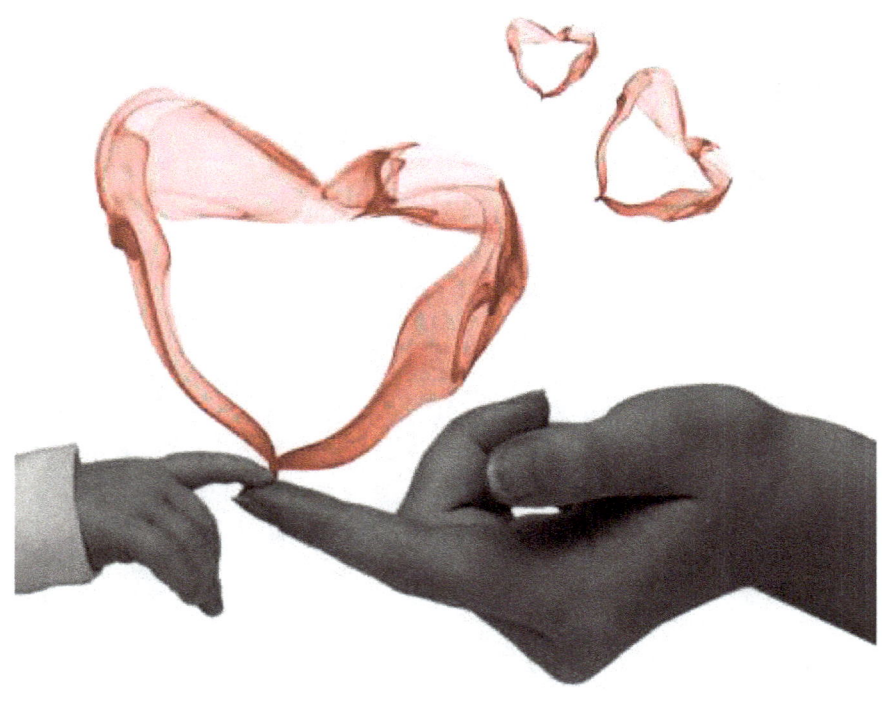

A Mother's Heart

Several years ago, I was blessed to interview my grandmother Mamie Bryant. I was interested in learning some family history and insight into her life in the early 1900's. I was more interested, however, in learning about my mother, her oldest child. My mother was born in the 1920's. She is the oldest of sixteen children born to Mamie and Bishop Bryant. Her father was a hard-working dirt farmer who lived in the red dirt of East Texas. Her mother worked and did what most of the women of that day did. They worked in the fields, made quilts, canned food for the winter, washed clothes with lye soap and had a bunch of children.

They called my mother "B." I'm not sure anyone knows where that name originated. She is still called "B" by her sisters and brothers. She is called "Aunt B" by her hoard of nieces and nephews. We, my siblings and I, simply call her Momma.

Grandmother's first words to me about my mother were, "She was a nice girl, and I really mean that." She went on to say, "She got saved when she was six years old. People thought she was playing, but she really got saved." Then she said, "She really loved her daddy, and she was a big help with her sisters and brothers."

Mother was blessed to complete high school at the small segregated country school. As Mother tells it, it was her heart's desire to be a nurse. After high school, she found herself living in Oklahoma City during World War II and working at a military installation. It was in Oklahoma during the war that she met a young soldier. They met, and they married.

The first of their eight children was born in August of 1945. I came along five years later. I am the fifth child. I guess you could say things were getting crowded when I came along. From my earliest recollection, I have always felt special. I thought that special feeling was unique to me. I later discovered that Mom has an uncanny ability to make several people feel special at the same time. Perhaps it was in the way that she would pull us to the side and whisper in our ear that we had a special ability or gift.

As I look back, I can see that she was bending us in the direction that she thought best utilized our personality and our abilities. Mother had a very unique perspective of her children. She saw us as a gift from God. She dedicated each of us back to God for His use and service. With that understanding, our lives revolved around church, Christian living and work. It did not take me long to realize that Mother, and Father for that matter, was totally committed to serving God. They were not committed out of a sense of duty to God, but out of their love for God.

One of the dynamic attributes of Mother is that she is a teacher. She took every opportunity to teach us lessons on life and living. She wanted us to excel at everything we undertook. When we were involved in programs at church for

Christmas or Easter, she wanted us to be the best presenter. She taught us how to stand, hold our hands together, look at the audience, and speak loudly and clearly. She made us learn those speeches, even if she had to use a switch. We sang with the children's choir and were in the plays. Vacation Bible School was a must. It goes without saying that we were in Sunday School every Sunday morning and in church every time the church doors were opened.

It was important to Mother that we all had a firm foundation of Christian instruction. Her instructions and training, however, went far beyond the church. Mother had six boys before a girl was born into the family. Mother decided that she would teach us boys all the things that one would normally think would be tasks for girls. Consequently, we all had to wash clothes, clean house, and cook. Mother's idea was to teach us to be self sufficient. I remember taking loads of clothes to the washateria. We were taught to make cornbread from scratch, cut up a chicken, fry it and make the gravy as well. By the time each of us left home, we knew how to cook for real.

Mother also had the idea that each of us would learn how to play the piano. So, off to piano lessons we went. She went all out with a real piano teacher who made us read music and perform at recitals. Mother was determined that we would be special. She received some criticism for being too strict on her boys. That did not deter her from her conviction that she had to mold us into productive citizens. While instructing us was something that she did almost daily, Mother also excelled at encouraging and assisting. She had the ability to discern the differences in our personalities. She seemed to know exactly what to say to each of us to encourage us to believe in God and to believe that we could make a difference. I was quite young when she would say, "You have wisdom, and you will be my counselor."

Even to this day, she will call me and ask my opinion on matters as her advisor. She has done so for many years. I know that she has spoken into the lives of all her children with words of encouragement. All of us have heard her voice when things were difficult. Mother has gone much further than encouraging us with her words. She is always ready to assist whenever there are times of sickness or challenges of any kind.

I believe God has honored her desire to be a nurse. She has labored tirelessly to assist ill family members and non family members alike. If you are sick, just call her. She has a remedy in store for you. In fact, it is likely that she has some medicines, herbs, or supplements in that special closet that everyone knows where it is but will not enter. We tell her that we are going to report her to the authorities for practicing medicine without a license.

If I were asked what was most impressive about Mother, I would say it is her love and care for her family. Her husband was definitely the number one priority. Close behind is her children. Mother was always working and engaged in helping others. She was quite involved in church activities, but we were never far out of her sight. Mother got licensed as a beautician. She had my dad build a beauty shop behind our house, so she could work and watch us. She would be in the shop frying hair and at the same time would observe us trying to sneak off to play down the street. She would walk out of the shop while hair was drying to check to see if we were working on our assignments.

When everything is said about my mother Ormie B. Martin, we cannot overlook the one thing that everyone agrees on about her. She is a woman of prayer and a friend of God. My earliest memories are of Mother telling us about Jesus. She emphasized the importance of giving our lives to Him, so we could go to heaven and miss hell. She told us of the goodness of Jesus and the power of prayer. We observed how she lived her life as a model of Christian living and faith in God. When we were sick and had no health insurance, she would doctor on us and pray the prayer of faith. We saw the power of God demonstrated through her prayer and obedience. If there was one thing we knew for sure that was that God is real and He saves, heals and works on behalf of those who love Him.

During the Vietnam War, she had five sons who were eligible to be drafted and sent to the war zone. There were so many young men who were killed, maimed and psychologically damaged by that war. Mother declared, "I did not raise my sons for Uncle Sam's army to get killed, wounded and damaged. I raised them to serve in God's army." Although some of us received notices from the government to serve, none of us ever did. Mother would take those notices to God and plead her case before Him, and He heard her cry. If you would talk to her, she could tell you of miracle after miracle that God did for our family.

Mother's modeling of Christian living showed us how a wife functions under the authority of her husband with love and respect. She showed us what the God kind of love is that exemplified itself fully as she gave herself to dad's care in the latter years of his life. She showed us how to serve in the church and to follow the leadership that God placed over her. She showed us what a woman of discretion is.

There is no other mother in the world like Ormie B. Martin. All of her children have risen, and we all call her blessed. She has blessed us.

The One I Adore

The Mary Robinson Story
by
La'Charee Tyqueisha Robinson

A Mother's Heart

My mother has been just that and more to me. She's been a mother, a friend, a supporter, and a provider. She instilled in me the tools and morals I need to survive throughout life. She taught me so much, such as the importance of honesty, self-respect and confidence, how to respect my elders and peers and even simple things like how to chew with my mouth closed. I wouldn't trade her for any other mother in the world. My mom and I haven't always had the best relationship, but I love, respect, and cherish her just as anyone else would his or her mother. She's smart, caring, courageous, intelligent, strong-willed and funny. This wonderful woman's name is Mary.

This big journey began when I was born on August 28, 1990. She gave birth to a beautiful healthy baby girl: me. While in labor, the doctor announced that she was ten centimeters dilated and told her not to push because she was progressing rapidly. She responded, "I'm not!!!" The nursed decided to switch her to another delivery bed and during that time I was still coming out without her pushing. Before the nurses could completely get her to the next bed, I was out. I was in such a rush that she never really had to push; I came out willingly.

Every time my mother tells this story, I think, "I was so eager to come out because I wanted to finally see this strong human being that has been carrying me for nine months." Ten depending on how you count. She says that all of her deliveries were a piece of cake. She has four children by the way. She had no medication whatsoever, especially for pain. She didn't want her babies to come out all drugged up. I could never really find myself believing that her deliveries were so easy. But then I thought either she was lying or this just goes to show how strong of a woman she really is. Later, I realized that she wasn't lying; she is really strong. Sometimes, I envy her because I wish I could be as strong as she.

While in the hospital, she decided to let my older sister, Chasha, name me. I don't know why or even how my sister came up with the name "La'Charee Tyqueisha Robinson." Now, don't get me wrong. I love my name, but Tyqueisha? Come on now, Chasha! All through middle school and high school, I was made fun of because of my middle name. I don't know how my mother knew, but she did. I guess it was her mother's instinct. She sat me down one day and said to me, "Don't sweat the small stuff, and don't feed into the negativity. Your name is very unique, and no one else in the world has a name like yours. And anyone that talks about your name secretly wants your name." From that day forward, every time someone told me that my name was weird, ghetto, or just plain old ugly, I just laughed it off and killed them with kindness.

My mother always told me that no matter what someone does to me, big or small, if I treat them kind they will either regret doing me wrong or they will feel ten times worse than they made me feel. Although in today's world I find that hard to do, I do try my best. I look around today at my peers, and it weakens my heart because I know that most of them are so blind to things, such as being kind and strong and having self-respect because they don't have parents or role models in their lives to teach them these things. I'm grateful and honored to say that I have a parent that has taught me these things and so much more.

Some parents I know today don't teach their kids morals and values because they claim they don't have time or they're working, etc. My mom has been through so much in her life, such as divorce, heartache, deaths in the family, living paycheck to paycheck and having to take time and find a way to make ends meet. But through all that, she always found time to make sure she taught us what we needed to know, and that's why we've turned out to be decent kids today.

When I was nine years old, my mom and dad had been married for a little over fifteen years. But what seemed like the perfect marriage went all wrong. Disgustingly to say, my dad disobeyed his vows and stepped out on my mom and their marriage for another woman. My little brother, who has the same dad as I, was seven years old at that time. As a child, the worst thing that could happen is seeing a parent walk out on you and your family, especially for me, because I was such a daddy's girl.

Through it all, I can't recall one time that I saw my mom cry. The only time I did see her cry was when my brother and I were crying. Other than that, I never saw a tear leave her face. Even in the moments when she was crying because we were, she still stayed strong enough to comfort us and told us not to cry because everything was going to be just fine. I worried so much that I wouldn't ever see my dad again and him not being in my little brother's life or my life anymore. I remember my mom telling us, "If he loves you, then he will come to see you, but if he doesn't, then don't worry because I will always love you."

Some people may see something wrong with telling their nine and seven year old children something like this, but I don't. I'm thankful that my mom told us the truth instead of telling us that he loves us and would for sure come to see us if she knew he wouldn't. She didn't feed us lies and get our hopes up for something that she knew wouldn't happen. Most parents today use lies to comfort their kids, but I find the truth much more comforting than a lie because a lie will hurt you in the long run and that's what my mom instilled in me. She never lied to us, and she taught us to be honest and truthful to others no what the situation is.

My mom and dad went through horrible, long, ridiculous court battles for my little brother and me. After everything was over, my mom was ordered full custody, and my dad could only have us on the weekends. At first, it was kind of weird going to see my dad at a new house, in a new neighborhood, and with his "girlfriend." But my mom ensured us that we were only there to spend time with our dad, nothing more and nothing less. The times that our dad didn't come to get us for whatever reason, my mom made sure that we were okay and found something fun for us to do so that it would take our minds off of him not coming to see us. Since all this happened, my dad hasn't been in our lives as much and on top of that, he moved to Chicago when I was fourteen. But at that age, I didn't let it affect me because I knew I still had my mom. As far as I'm concerned, she's my mother and my father, and that's just fine with me.

In 2004, my grandma (my mom's mother) got really sick. It hurt my family deeply because she was the seed of the family. Anytime something happened within the family, she was the only one that could make it all better. It was a long battle, and in April of 2004, she passed. My mom took it very hard because they were like best friends. I've never seen my mom so hurt and out of it. Everyone just fell apart, and my big happy family was no longer. My family split up and started fighting; we even discontinued getting together for holidays. It took my mom a while to get past things, but as soon as she did, she felt she had a mission to get the family back together. She called everyone trying to hash out whatever problems were going on throughout the family. She tried so hard to carry on my grandma's will. Slowly, but surely, the family started to make amends, and we started to have family gatherings again.

My mom is one of the strongest people I know to have come back from something like this and try to take on a family like mine and get us back together. I don't know what she had to say or do to make it happen, but it did. I can almost guarantee it wasn't nice, but whatever it was it worked. Her soft and smart words are powerful beyond measure, and I hope to one day be exactly like that.

When I got to high school, everything got so much harder for my mother. Because of her divorce from my dad, she didn't have much help with me, but she did what she could. She found a way to make ends meet. She worked a full-time job and was on welfare just to make sure my cousin, my brother, and I had clothes and shoes for school, not to mention lunch money every day. She was extremely hardworking and dedicated and all because of her kids. She made sure we had food on the table and a roof over our head. We always had a great Christmas, and we always had a costume for Halloween. Even if it was a homemade costume, she made sure that we had one. She has gone over and above what a mother is expected to do for her child. She's phenomenal.

In my sophomore year of high school at Artesia High, I got kicked out. I was always late to classes or ditching and not doing homework. She tried her best to stay on me and make sure that I was doing the things I was supposed to be doing. But just like any other teenager, I had my sneaky ways of going about things. But on the day I got kicked out, all of my sneaky and cocky ways were turned into fear. The school called my mom to come pick me, and I was terrified. I remember the ride home was so silent that you could hear a pin drop. That was one of the scariest moments of my life, and I just knew for sure that when we arrived at home I was going to get beat.

Well, when we got home, I didn't get a whooping, but I also didn't get anything else: no TV, no phone, and no friends over. I couldn't even go to the front door. I got double chores, and everyone made fun of me. At the time, I thought my mom hated me for doing this. She sat back and let my family talk about me, curse me out and all kinds of stuff. Now that I'm older, I know that it was just tough love. If she didn't show me tough love, I would not be the person I am today, and I thank my mom for that.

A few weeks later, my mom, my brother and I moved to Victorville. I started a new high school, and everything started to get a lot better. I was getting good grades and was attending classes like I should. I found new friends that I hung out with on a regular basis. After being there for a year,

I got accustomed to all the teachers, staff and all my peers. Everything was going great. Until one day a girl decided to try and bully me. I let her slick and throat-cutting words pass by me all day. But at the end of the day, she decided to come in my face.

Now, my mom always taught me to defend myself when necessary- no matter who, what, or where. So that's what I decided to do. I defended myself! When the school contacted my mom, she was surprised that I had actually put my hands on someone at school. It was a bittersweet moment for her. She was glad that I defended myself, but she was disappointed that I had defended myself in that manner. She told me to do unto others as I would want them to do unto me. At that time, I was just mad that the girl came up to my face and started to be very nasty with me, so I reacted the first way that came to my mind. I never really understood why my mom would always tell me that until I got older. With all of this going on, she decided that it was best for me to transfer to another school, so I did.

The next semester, I started at an alternative education school. It was my last semester of high school. I met new friends and got into more drama. Not as serious as before, but it was still drama. I dropped out and never ended up graduating. My mom was furious. She saw that I was changing for the worst, so she tried her best to reshape and mold me into doing better. She told me that I should never get wrapped up into drama for anyone. Friends aren't going to get me where I need to be; an education will get me where I need to be. She told me to stay focused no matter what obstacles come my way. If I have faith in God and believe that He will make it better, then it will be. I knew that I had broken her heart, but she still stood tall and gave me words of wisdom and made sure that I knew which paths I had to choose from and the consequences of those paths.

Life started to get a lot better from then on. When was nineteen, I became pregnant, and she was ecstatic because I gave her a chance at having a granddaughter. At that time, she had three grandsons and was anxious to have a granddaughter. When I was four months pregnant, we all found out that it was a girl. My mom was more excited than I had ever seen her before. She was going to have a granddaughter. She treated me like I was a princess. "Don't carry this, don't carry that, sit down, don't move, you don't have to bend over or reach up for that, I will do it." I was on cloud nine. She did everything for me while I was pregnant, and she made sure I didn't go beyond my means or did anything I wasn't supposed to be doing.

The doctor first told me that my due date was on September 5th, which is my mom's birthday. I remember her being so happy. She told me, "Great, now you can have me and the baby's birthday party together." Little did she know that was never going to happen- LOL. Well, my daughter didn't come on the fifth; she came on the seventh of September. I named her Kimara T'sehai Faith White. My mom helped with any and everything that I needed for Kimara, strollers, car seats, clothes and diapers; whatever I needed she made sure I had. She wasn't doing these things because she knew Kimara needed it; she was doing to help me, and I appreciate every little thing she did. Most parents don't go to a high extent to get things for their grandkids, but my mom did. She was amazing.

When I turned twenty-one, I got my own apartment with my boyfriend and daughter. My mom was proud that I was starting to get my life together and started to grow into the young woman that she had hoped for me to be. She supported me and tried to help me in every aspect of that. I didn't have a car at the time, so she would help me with things like taking us to doctor's appointments, taking us grocery shopping, or when she couldn't take us places, she gave me money to take the bus. She was so caring, and whenever I needed her, she was there.

I'm now twenty-two, and I've recently had another child, a son named Aaron Michael White II. He's nine months old, and my mom supports me just as she did with my first child. When I'm tired and need a break from the kids, she will take care of them for a couple days. When I need to go to school, she will watch them for me. Even when I just want to go out with my boyfriend, she will be there for me and watch the kids. I appreciate her so much and have the upmost respect for her no matter what we go through.

My mom and I haven't always seen eye to eye; in fact, we almost never see eye to eye. But whatever she tries to tell me or get me to do, I respect it, and I take it into consideration, whether it's about my kids, about my friends or relationship, or even just about my personal health. I know that she just wants the best for me and my kids, and that's why she drills me about every little thing. She doesn't want her kids to make the mistakes that she has made in the past, so she always tells us, "Learn from my mistakes."

When I was young, I never knew why my mom did the things she did to or for us. I didn't know why she would whoop us or punish us or tell us we couldn't do this or that, or we could only go here or there. But now that I'm older, and I have children of my own, I understand exactly why she did the things she did.

She wanted to raise us with tough love and teach us to be all we could be. She taught us to always try our hardest at whatever we wanted in life. She taught us how to choose our paths and how to recognize the right and wrong. She taught us to be patient and kind to others, but not let anyone take our kindness for weakness. She taught me and my sister how to be good women and taught my brothers how to be good men. For a woman to have four kids, work her whole life, support us, care for us, make sure we had clothes on our backs and food on our table, and do it all alone, I applaud her. She had no help at all besides the Lord up above. If that isn't a strong phenomenal woman, then I don't know what is.

Throughout my life, I strive to be at least half the woman she is today. Everyone I know loves, cherish, and respects her to the fullest, and that is how I want people to feel towards me. I can't imagine life without my mom, and I hate to even think of losing her in my life.

Mommy, you are the reason I am the woman I am today, and I hope I have made you at least half as proud as I am of you. I wouldn't trade you for the world, and I wish to become just like you. I love you.

Ups and Downs, but Together We STAND TALL

The Maisha D. Hartfield Story
by
Eyounae Hayes

Maisha and Eyounae

A Mother's Heart

A Mother's Heart

For the longest time, I had been trying to figure out how life would be if I were a twin, not realizing that I've had one since the day I was born. That might sound crazy, and I know you're wondering what in the world could I possibly be talking about. Well, like any other relationship, my mother and I have had our share of ups and downs, but there is no one in this world I would have rather shared those moments with than my mother.

As a kid, I didn't want for anything. I thought it was the coolest thing ever to have a mom that would do literally ANYTHING for her kids. I remember playing house pretending to be my mom. I started walking like her, talking like her, handling business like her, even yelling at my pretend kids like her. She was my superwoman.

When I was twelve, I unexpectedly got sick from breaking out in rashes covering my entire body, to super bad headaches, to my hair falling out uncontrollably, even all the way down to having terrible mood swings. I mean I was twelve for crying out loud. That was a lot to handle, especially being so young. I was rushed back and forth to different hospitals, and no one had any answers for my mom. It was becoming sickening to her as a parent to see me suffer, and there was really nothing that she could do, but she NEVER gave up.

She started giving me her own doses of medications, trying out new medications that would work for a while then stop; she was doing everything in her power to help her baby girl get well.

Out of all the doctor appointments I have been to in my lifetime, there is one that I remember so clearly. My mom sat right in front of me and the doctor and cried saying that if she could be the one dealing with this she would. She said she would cut all her hair off (FOR ME) because she didn't care about hair. (She knew that bothered me most). She would do anything to see her daughter well.

Since no one wanted to give her answers, she started doing her own research, and as crazy as it sounds, my little cousin had the same symptoms at the same time as I. When my little cousin's mom found out, she referred my mom and me to the doctor her daughter was going to. I ended up going there as well. Dr. McCurdy changed our lives. She cared for me with love, and she comforted my mom because she knew how hard it was on her. After a few doctor appointments, I was diagnosed and FINALLY began treatment for "Juvenile Rheumatoid Arthritis," a condition I would have to deal with for the rest of my life.

Yes, it was hard. I felt different from the rest. I felt awkward. I couldn't believe I wasn't 'normal' anymore. I couldn't believe I wouldn't be able to do a lot of the things that I've loved doing for all these years. I was first put on a steroid used to control the swelling and the rashes. I gained a lot of weight. I just couldn't believe this was happening. I remember crying to my mom and being mad all the time. I would always ask her, "Why me?"

She always made me feel like I was beautiful and told me it didn't matter what people said. My mom, my savior, my biggest cheerleader has been with me EVERY SINGLE STEP OF THE WAY! Even until this very day, she gives me the comfort and love I need. Now don't get me wrong. We do have our share of downs.

When I was in high school, I thought I knew everything. I thought I had it all figured out, and nobody couldn't tell me anything…and I mean NOTHING! Well, my mom and I got into a fight. I really wouldn't call it a fight because we all know who would have won, but instead I'll call it an altercation. One day, I just decided to leave and not say where I was going. But my phone bill wasn't paid (if it's one thing I hate is having my cell phone off).

So, to get my point across, I just wasn't going to tell her anything. When I came back into the house, she came into my room and asked where I was. I thought I was a bad little something and wasn't going to answer. When she stepped to me, I immediately put my hands up because I was not a fan of getting hit, especially not in my face, so I was just looking out for myself. Of course, she got mad and created a huge scene yelling, screaming, and trying to hit me. I got out of there as fast as I could. I ran to my friend's house and called my god-mom to come and get me. I stayed with them for a few days until I decided I would go live with my dad because I couldn't keep missing school.

Living with my dad didn't last long. I just wasn't comfortable with him. He didn't do the things my mom did. He was cheap and just didn't have that motherly love that my mom gave me, but I stuck it through with him just to show my mom that I "thought" I didn't need her. I eventually ended up going home. I really don't even remember how or when I got there, but I know I made it in the house alive. At that point in my life, I was just angry and lashing out; I wanted that mother-daughter perfect relationship that I saw my friends have with their moms.

My mom never called me "baby, sweetie, hun," and I hated it. I was never a fast little girl. But if I asked for something and didn't get it right then and there, I was literally mad at the entire world and didn't want to talk to anyone. My mom had a problem with that, and now that I look back, I see how crazy I was when I knew if she had it she would do anything in this world for me. But that was just me being a brat, but can you blame me?

She had spoiled me my entire life. I didn't know how to act when times got hard or when a man had come into the picture. I just wanted it to be us, like it had been for the longest. I felt like I was losing a piece of me, but I didn't know how to tell her, so I let my attitude get the best of me. It got to the point where I felt like I had lost the loving, down-to-earth mom that would do anything for her kids. How could that be? Someone that would go to the moon and back for me really switched up on me. I didn't know how to handle it. I couldn't stand the man that she was with. I wouldn't speak to him, and I hated to see him in my house.

Now I know I am not one to judge if my mom wants to be with the "world's dumbest human" and she's happy. That's her business, and I'm going to support her 100% just as she does me with my crazy, no words to describe relationship that I'm in right now. Besides, my baby brother's dad wasn't half bad once I actually gave him chance. I was mad at my mom for a lot of different reasons but even after me moving with my dad (which I felt like I let her down. How could I up and run to someone that hadn't been there for me my whole life?), not speaking to my mom, and saying a lot of hurtful things to her, she still had my back.

Something so life changing for my mother and me was being a second-year student here at Cal State Stanislaus and finding out my mom was about to have another baby. I had known for a long time, but I didn't say anything to anyone because I just didn't want to believe what was going on, and I was quite embarrassed. Once my older brother confirmed it, I just felt empty. I didn't want anything to do with my mom...NOTHING! How dare she bring another baby into this world when I'm nineteen years of age with no car!

I just couldn't wrap my mind around what was going on. I was rather bothered and didn't speak to my mom for months, only if she spoke to me first. There were many days I was hungry or just needed that motherly advice, but I wouldn't go to her if it was the last thing left to do on earth. I'm just stubborn and always want things my way. I was hurting because I was so used to telling my mom everything. That's just how I am.

A little before she had the baby, she texted me because she was very upset. Then, a little after, she called me. And as she spoke, she began to cry telling me how much me not speaking to her hurt and how she knew that I would be upset and if she could have gotten an abortion she would have. But that wasn't an option for her because she would have lost her life by doing so (due to medical reasons). I couldn't believe I was so selfish to have wanted her to kill my little brother or worse herself. I seriously couldn't imagine life without my baby brother (Junie). It's actually fun having a new baby being that my little sister (Tank) is thirteen. She has her own little crew. She goes skating every weekend, to the mall, and to Knott's Berry Farm. She definitely isn't worried about hanging with me. I guess I had never looked at the blessing God sent by creating my baby brother.

I explained to my mom after she had the baby that I was really upset because I felt she wasn't going to be able to be a grandmother to our kids (my siblings & I). But she assured me that if I had a kid tomorrow she would be there for me without a shadow of a doubt. I had nothing to worry about.

Now that I am older, away from home, in college, and doing my own thing, I see just how much I appreciate how strong of a mother I was blessed with. I now see that she doesn't have to call me "baby, sweetie, hun" for me to know she loves me. Plus, that just isn't in her personality.

She's a tough cookie. I can't lie, and even though her attitude can be a bit much to handle at times, I really wouldn't trade her for the anything in this world. I know most people have a problem saying they need people. Even as much as I say when I'm mad, "I don't need you…I don't care about this and that," well let me tell you…I'm lying, and I need my mom.

If it's one thing that I've learned from her it's how to be a "go-getter." She showed me that Mommy can be Daddy, carry the world on her back, and still make it happen without that father figure. I never had the chance to make poor decisions because I watched my mom "do it" my whole life. I know a lot of people blame not having a dad as an excuse to be low lives or just to make stupid choices. Well, my mom and I are living proof that it's possible.

My mom graduated college (pregnant with my little sister) and worked for as long as I can remember. I only know how to "succeed." It's in her blood, so you know it's in mine. I can't wait to one day have kids and give them all the love and support my mom has given me over the years and even a good chewing out when they act up. Lord knows I got a lot of them ... even until this very day. My mom is living proof that there are no excuses in life and anything you set your mind to can be done.

It's crazy. All my life, I had searched and searched for a relationship like I saw other people have with their moms, not knowing that I had been living the all-American "mother-daughter" relationship my entire life. My walk, my talk, my attitude, my choice of words, my character, and my sense of humor, all the way down to my body frame are all compliments of my momma.

Maisha D. Hartfield, you know I always say this but God knew what He was doing when He paired us up. We are a match made in heaven. I love you forever and ever, my queen.

Unconditional Love

The Franzette Kyles Story
by
Jourdan Jovel

Franzette and Jourdan

A Mother's Heart

My relationship with my mom has always been open and honest; for instance, if something was going to hurt like taking a shot, my mom would tell me about it beforehand.

My mom does not punish me because she is angry. If she is angry, she tells me to go to another room. While I am in the other room, she calms down and thinks of the right punishment. After she punishes me, she asks me if I think the punishment was fair. If my mom thinks that the punishment was wrong, she will ask for forgiveness, even if I didn't think it was wrong.

Whenever I am having a problem, I talk to my mom about it. She always seems to know what I am going through and gives great advice. She helps when it comes to school, friends, or anything really.

I know that she loves me, and she knows that I love her. Almost every day of my life, she tells me that she loves me and that she thanks God that I was born. She says that I am a gift to her.

My mom also stops whatever she is doing to spend time with me unless she is witnessing to other people because I am more important than anything else that she is doing.

When I was younger, every Friday, my mom and I always had mother-daughter days. We would go to the park, the museum, or out to fancy restaurants; it was fun every time. One time, when I was a toddler, my mom and I were at a restaurant where music was playing, and I asked my mom to dance. We danced around all of the waiters and waitresses even though there wasn't a dance floor and we weren't supposed to dance, but she loved me enough.

My mom also taught me how to skate. It has been a while since I last skated, so I am not as good. She was also teaching me how to skateboard.

She taught how to read when I was two, how to do multiplication when I was four, and how to do division when I was five. One time, I was in a school where I wasn't getting a good education, and they wouldn't let me transfer to another school district. My mom contacted every school board member, the mayor, each city council member, and those who were running for those positions. When they still wouldn't let me get transferred, she threatened to bring in the media and the president too. That was when they let me transfer. She has always been this serious about my education.

My mom also tells me her mistakes because she doesn't want to make me think that she is perfect, and she does not want me to make the same mistakes.

For almost my whole life, it has just been me and my mom. As a single mother, I think that she has done a great job raising me. My mom has also taught me to embrace and appreciate both of my heritages, as my dad is Hispanic and my mother is African American.

My mom has also brought me up in church since I was three weeks old because she wanted me to have the same spiritual foundation that she was given when she was little.

I think that my mom is smart, wise, and just amazing. She is a wonderful woman. And I want to be like her when I grow up. Sure she is not perfect, but I don't care. She is still amazing in my eyes, and I love her.

A Mother's Heart

An Irreplaceable Bond

The Eyana A. (Williams) Flemister Story
by
Khalil Malik Flemister

Eyana and Khalil

A Mother's Heart

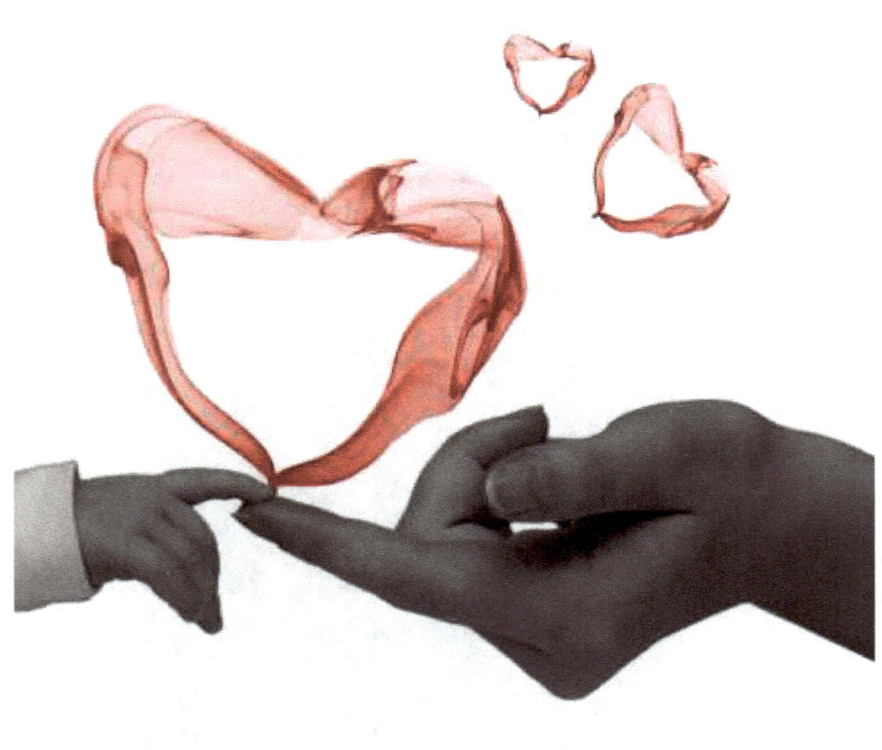

A mother's love is unlike anything on this world. The bond between a mother and her child is stronger than any metal, more complex than any puzzle, and more beautiful than any piece of art.

When you look up the definition of mother, it is simply defined as a female parent. But to me, there is much more than that to my mom. She deserves much more credit. She is a strong, caring, and independent woman, who with the help of my father, has devoted eighteen years plus to raising me. The amazing thing about Eyana Flemister is that not only is she my mother, but she is also my motivator and my teacher. Making her proud is my ultimate goal, and I won't stop until I succeed.

My dad did a great job of teaching me how to carry myself with respect and integrity as a young man, but my mom consistently reminded me that it was only the half of it, and that I also had to be a gentleman and treat women with respect and compassion. From a young age, I was taught that I was never to disrespect, hit, or call a woman out of her name.

Even though my mom is big on being a gentleman, she also stressed the importance of being independent and being able to cook, clean, and wash without having to rely on a woman, just the basics that I would need to take care of myself.

One thing my mom has a habit of doing is asking me a series of repetitive questions on a daily basis. One of them that sticks out is, "How are your grades?" Even though my grades are good, that question always gets me nervous. The fact that my mom does care about my grades and how I'm doing shows me that she wants me to succeed and get a good education. She always rumbles off, "You're going to college" and "You're going to do better than what I did." My mom is an intelligent woman. She proved to me that even with a family, work, and responsibilities she could go back to school and continue her education.

When it comes to responsibilities, my mother is on my back constantly. She tells me that I have to be on top of things because as an adult the real world won't wait for me. She tells me that she wants me to be responsible and be able to take care of myself when she's not around. We'll joke around a lot, but she'll tell me when I need to be serious and make sure my maturity is there when needed for serious situations.

When I hear my mom talk about her childhood with my grandma, I learn about all the picnics, talks, walks, and time spent and shared between them. You can hear the love and respect she has for her mother. And in my head, I have these crazy thoughts because my mother and I had all the same picnics, talks, walks, and time spent and shared between us. And I wonder if she knows that I feel the same exact way she is describing her love for her mom.

Even though I've gotten older and don't need as much in-face attention as I did when I was younger, it's still good to know my mom is still keeping an eye on me. I understand that she can't always be there like she was when I was a kid, but without that same affection here and there, even at 17 years old, I wouldn't feel the same. And I admit even though my mom doesn't feel this way, I'm truly a mama's boy!

Don't get me wrong. My mom and I have a great relationship, but everything wasn't always good. We do argue and disagree on many things, but that's just two hard-headed people who are just trying to get their point across. There have been heated arguments where foul words have been used and tears have been shed. But at the end, it has brought us closer, and we talked and expressed how we truly feel and try to get everything off our chests.

I've been playing sports all my life and usually I'm used to my having random strangers and people looking at me and spectating at my games and meets. But when I spot my mom in the stands, it's a different story. I get this sense of nervousness and panic because I don't want to disappoint her and perform badly. When she is there, I have a little more motivation to warm up a little harder, run a little faster and take the meet or game even more seriously, just because I want to make her proud. Her support and approval mean a lot to me.

Everyone knows that my mom is very protective, sometimes too protective to the point that sometimes it's nerve wrecking. I try to explain to her that she has to eventually let go and let me be, but she gives me the excuse that "I'm her baby, her only child." Even though I understand where she is coming from, I try to explain to her that I'm getting older and have to learn and experience things for myself. After telling her, still I never fail to hear a response like, "You'll understand when you have children of your own" or simply a sharp stare.

Even though she is a nice and laid-back woman, don't let that fool you. My mom always talks about how the only person you should fear is the Lord above and how she is pretty tough. At first, you think she's just talking but after hearing a few stories from her childhood, I learned that she was a tom boy and was indeed pretty tough. Take it from me, I've felt a couple of her punches, and there was some force behind them. I guess that's a good thing in helping me stay focused and disciplined. But I can say that my mom has both mental and physical toughness.

My mother always asks me if I felt that she did a good job as a mother. I can honestly say she did a great job. I mean no one is perfect, and people make mistakes, but she did everything in her will to make sure I lived a good life. With both my mom and dad in my life, it was great, and I'm grateful for that because I know a lot of kids who don't have that. I never had to live a tough life and struggle. I got things that I needed and wanted. Yes, I got exposed to things that I would have chosen not to see, but I'm thankful that my mom and dad put in work and time for better opportunities.

Out of all my fears in life, losing my mother is the biggest. Just thinking about it scares me. It is a concept I can't grasp yet. You have the saying, "You don't know what you have until it's gone" and it's true. I know I have taken her for granted so many times, and I realized how much I need and depend on her being here. My dad may be the back bone of my family, but my mother is our rock and the glue that holds us together. I've learned to enjoy the little things that come with my mother and try to make the best memories possible.

I'm surprised that I had the guts to actually talk about our relationship. I'm to say that Eyana Alicia Flemister is my mother. I know it may sound cliché, but I feel that I have the best mom in the world. I'm glad that I was blessed with someone who truly loves and cares for me. And I know I can talk and confide with her and no judgment will be passed. I can count on her to be there and have my back no matter how bad the situation is. Hopefully, when she reads this, she'll recognize how much I love, care, and need her in my life.

A Mother's Heart

Dedication to My Mother

Dear mother of mine, this is an ode to you.

Seventeen years and I still can't understand how a mother can care for her child like you do.

To be there, to care, like you do.

To guide and love like you do.

That warm embrace can force any storm away.

And things return to normal like they are supposed to.

I'm not just trying to rhyme or waste time.

Because each word was chosen because they perfectly describe you.

The jokes, your laugh, and that motherly affection that brightens up my day as they're supposed to

One day, I hope you open your eyes and realize that I wear my heart on my sleeve for you

I took my emotions and feeling and mixed in admiration and came up with this ode to you.

Forgiveness

The Francine Duff Story
by
Audrey Albrecht

A Mother's Heart

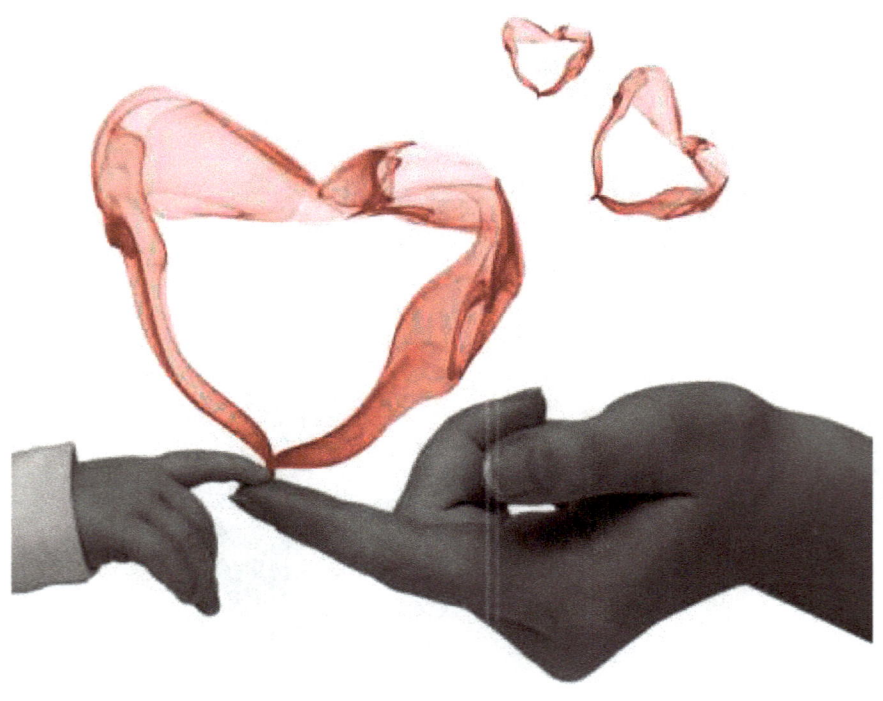

I woke up to a cloudy morning, a Saturday lost as the storm came in. Outside, I could feel the stillness. Opaque clouds hung closely to the horizon. This was not a day for unpacking as I had hoped for.

How could this be? I am now fifty-something. Yet, I still avoid a truth which lives quietly around my perceived reality.

My Francine, I am ashamed to admit that this is one of the few times I have written your name since I cannot remember when. After shuffling two small boxes from storage to garage for over the past eight years, I now am a captive of the weather and forced to look inside. No more moving it along. My husband and I have moved into our dream house. I intend to deal with you there, to finally love you.

My dad Leslie was the Mother Teresa of men. But his flaw was that he loved without any rules when it came to "her." Both my parents were of strict Latin Catholic backgrounds. They found common ground in their faith when they married. Dad was shy and once told my uncle that he decided to marry her because no one else would. How silly, Dad.

It was the 1950's; the plan for women was to marry, have a baby, and be happy. Define happy when you are unsure of who you are. She was so beautiful. He was defenseless.

A Mother's Heart

At seven or eight years old, I began to understand that some things just would never change. My sister, two years old than I, catered to my mom more than I did out of self preservation. My feisty nature was not good. I am the child of a chemically dependent person. I am the grandchild of co-dependent grandparents. My mom's parents looked away from her behavior. In doing so, they ruined her and all of us too. It was out of love as most co-dependency is.

Another portable meatloaf brought over by my grandparents and dishes done, away they went. And I was left there alone as she slept throughout my childhood. However, in her moments of being awake, she could be very difficult with which to engage. So most of the time, I spoke my mind and paid the price.

From time to time, I could hear my dad talking to his mom on the phone behind a half-closed door. He would say, "Mom, she does not want to do anything, except sleep. She throws rages if I don't do what she wants." It was as if he justified her behavior.

We rarely saw my dad's parents. I know he missed them as well as his brothers and sister. To my dad, that was the longest 50 miles away imaginable. Every family event, baseball game and holiday was a struggle. We always knew who would win.

In 1969, when man finally walked on the moon, my dad lost his parents only forty days apart. That loss changed the game again. He no longer had a tether to comfort him. It was just him and me. I begged him to leave Easter of 1970. He said that he would not. God would disapprove. That was the day I knew nothing would ever change.

Shock treatments were popular at that time. Francine had thirty of them. Whatever energy and original self may have existed in her was dumbed down. There was not much left. She was a drug seeker in failing health.

Seven years had passed without much change. By then, my dad has divorced her twice and remarried her again. Was God angry? If He wasn't, we were. I was ready to leave. I met my first husband. We married in three months time.

The first day I went to meet my future in-laws, I must have looked like a homeless person: unmatched and poor. We drove into the driveway of their beautiful home. I did not want to go. I was too embarrassed and timid. So, I sat on the porch. From the window I say Trudy, my mother-in-law to be. She was very in charge, very organized and very German. There she was, a mom, up and running. It was a little intimidating, yet fascinating. There she was doing all the 'mom' things and so filled with love for her family. In my heart, she was my first mom.

World War II was just another war; she was good at survival. She and a group of women walked from city to city in hope of finding food and shelter for two years. She was just a teenager living from day to day.

When my husband and I returned from our honeymoon, a drunk driver hit us head on going the wrong way on the freeway. Suddenly, I saw myself looking down from above. I was not in pain. My body lay there. *I must be dead,* I thought. At that moment, I heard an unspoken voice. It said that I could let go. There was peace beyond definition. That I do remember. In that moment, I knew our Creator in a way that sitting in a pew could never accomplish. In that time of twilight, I stayed in the Lord's care. I survived the crash, but I experienced brain trauma. I could not remember my husband or my name.

In the months that followed, Trudy took care of me. My in-laws took me out of the hospital. Hospitals to Trudy were places to die. She was determined to make me whole again.

Over the course of three years, she never let me down. We started with the basics: to walk, to remember and feel independent again. To this day, I have the utmost respect for her and her enduring love and patience. It has helped me to be a better mother, friend and person.

As I open Francine's boxes, I found the remnants of a scared and confused person. I looked through the Prayer books, loose ends and emptiness. I always felt guilty for loving Trudy more. I now can say it is not more love but more respect. In my life, I parented a parent and buried the emotional child that she was. But I am strong because of Trudy.

If you can love the things that are not perfect in life, you will find forgiveness. All moms aren't perfect. Love is a peace grantor, the way time is a healer.

.

A Mother's Heart

The Strength of One Woman

The Mary Ann Vines Story
by
Cathy Vines-Nichols

Mary and Her Children

A Mother's Heart

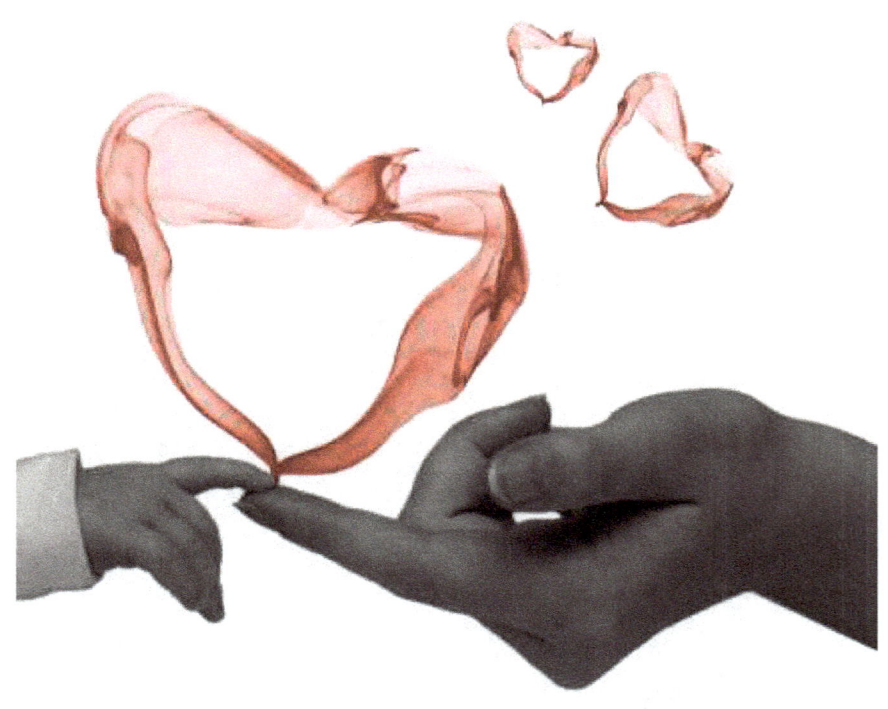

Mary (a.k.a. May) is the oldest of eight children. Her mother's name was Rosie Gullett. Her father's name was Seaborn Henderson, Jr. They met and married, and that union produced a baby girl they named Mary Ann Vines. She grew up in Texarkana, Texas and attended school there. Mary had two children: a daughter Joyce Anderson and a son Wayne Pittman.

Later in life, she met Roger Vines, Sr. They married and eleven children were added to their family. I bless God for a mother that has endured hardship going through life's journey. 'Going through' is what made her the tree that stands by the river of living water. Her roots go deep into the soil; her soil is her children and family. It is in her strength that we have been able to stand because of the prayers she and our father prayed. I remember the prayer was, "God, save all my children. Don't let one be lost. Keep them covered with your Holy Ghost in Jesus' name, Amen."

Mary is a prayer warrior, one that fights the good fight of faith. She has never given up on her family. She is all about family. She is that strong tower in her family, the oldest of eight. The number eight represents "one who abounds in strength' is "superabundant and fertile"; she is "oil." Eight as the day was over and above this perfect completion. Mary is a blessing to her thirteen children: (in order) Joyce Montgomery, Pastor Wayne Pittman, Rosie Marie Harvey, Roger Vines, Jr., Ronald Vines, Evang. Cathy Vines-Nichols,

Renee Vines, Tonie L. Vines, Melenia J. Vines, Kenneth D. Vines, Angela Vines (a.k.a. Love-Love), Kevin Vines, and the baby Ruthie Vines-Ruffin.

Mary is loyal to her family. Her trust is in the Lord. She is giving and will give you her last. She wants nothing but the best for her family. When there is a change in the atmosphere of her family, she is on it. She mixes no words in setting order (she speak what is on her mind, right or wrong). She will be heard.

Mary has the love and respect of her siblings: (in order) Albert Henderson, Justine Smith (a.k.a. Tina), Helen Williams (a.k.a. Aunt Boo), Dr. Francis Henderson-Solomon, James Henderson, Larry Henderson, and Willie Henderson. Mary, her sister Justine, and her brother Albert were very close. When Mary was moving to another part of town, it wasn't long before Tina and Albert would follow. They lived at least no more than five to ten minutes away from each other.

They did everything together. Mary and Tina were best friends. A day never went by without them calling each other on the phone. They would talk about three times a day just to hear each other's voice. They partied together. They could party, and Mary was a dancer. Oh!! this sister could hold her own. They shopped together. If the store had layaway, it was on. Back then, there was Swans in Oakland and Capwell's Department Store. Back then, layaway was a good thing.

Remember, she had thirteen children. Mary and her sister even dressed alike from the top to the tip of the shoes. They could not have been any closer. That is the love of one another in the family. They were two peas-in-a pod; they laughed and cried together.

And then a shift happened. Tina started going to Ephesians Church of God in Christ on 132nd St. in Los Angeles, CA where the pastor was Bishop E. E. Cleveland. A lady by the name of Mother Ellis was the cause of Tina changing her life. Tina became a prayer warrior and that pulled Mary in. Just like they partied together, they never lost a beat. They took their love for each other to the House of Worship. They dressed, danced (shouted), praised the Lord, and lifted up hands together in worship; they sang in the choir together, and I tell you Mary can sing. They shared so much love between the two of them until God had need of Tina to come home. And the way Mary handled it was as if she was walking and holding the hand of Jesus Himself. Yes, she cried, the tears flowed, each day for years, but Mary had thoughts of her sister; best friend was gone.

I saw in her a strength that just illuminated when she entered my presence. I now see what took her through- knowing the Christ. I watched her brother Albert and the relationship they have to this day. It is still the same each day- a phone call or a visit to one's home for dinner or driving to the mall just to sit or walk around with each other.

Uncle Albert used to come over to our house every day after work just to see May (Mary). He would stay for hours. They would embrace each other, laugh and talk. Then, Albert would walk to the driveway, lift the car's trunk open and play his music, etc. Then, he would go home. This was an everyday thing. That is love in action to this day.

Mary has a love that goes beyond mother, wife, friend, daughter, aunt, and cousin. What respect her sisters and brothers have for her. Mary is still that way toward her family, even when her brother James was called home. She displayed the strength of God when she once again was going through life without another sibling. But God showed Himself strong in her.

She had her own battle with breast cancer in 1999; she is a walking testimony. I get great joy when I see my mother go forth in praise. I remember her sitting on the side of her bed with a Bible in hand reading. Mary is a strong woman of faith, integrity, and strength. Our mother is the strength of the family. Yes, she can be strong willed at times, but you have to love her! LOL! I remember the love that she shared with her oldest grandson (my son) Edgar. Their relationship was a good one. He would call her and visit. They even went to church together. They would go out to dinner and do things together. When she heard that Edgar was in the hospital, she made the journey to Las Vegas, NV to be with him.

When she entered his room, I could see the love she had for him and the compassion of her grandson for her. At her seventy-fifth birthday party, he did a tribute in dance to her. It was awesome. In the hospital, the tears flowed and the hugs came. They talked and laughed for a while just because she has such love for her family. She had made it a point to be there for him. I bless God because she made the difference that day; the love gleamed from her eyes as she looked at him, and he was smiling back at her because Granny was there. Oh the joy she brought to him.

Two days later, he died. Yet again, the strength she has never failed her. What a woman! Oh just to be a woman like her! God will give you what you need when you need it. The joy she shared with him can't be replaced. Our mother is a woman of wisdom, integrity, strength. I see this the more I put pin to paper. There are fine qualities God has placed in her to give to her family. She really is all about family. She is the rock of this family.

For her sister Francis, Mary was sister and mother. When Francis was about 17 years of age, she lived with May. She treated me with love and like her own child, and whatever she said she meant and meant what she said. I remember her cooking, washing, cleaning, and praying for her family every day. She loves her family. All I can say is that she is the greatest sister/mother that anyone could ever have. I can see the great qualities she possesses that came down from our mother; our mother was a great woman of strength. My mother also had a strong mother, who lived to 94 years of age. She never turned anyone away who was in need. Rosie, my grandmother, was a woman of wisdom and integrity. She as the rock of stability kept us coming back to the center, which is family. Because of my grandmother, my mother is who she is, and I love my mother dearly.

Mommy and Me

The Wanda Clayton Story
by
Akayla Clayton

Wanda and Akayla

A Mother's Heart

A Mother's Heart

My mother and I have the best relationship ever. Don't get me wrong. It wasn't always as good as it is now, but it was never bad.

I was the second child born to my parents, four years after my brother. From the beginning, when my parents asked my brother if he liked me, he answered, "Yes." Then, he was asked what he wanted to do with me. His reply was, "Throw her in the trash." He eventually changed his mind and became my big brother!

While growing up, I was always a 'daddy's girl' and my brother was a 'mommy's boy.' My mom and my brother would do things together, and my dad and I would do things together. I always knew she loved me, but I didn't think I was her favorite.

When we were growing up, my mom was the most youthful, laid back, smartest, prettiest thing I had ever encountered. She never looked or acted like the other mothers in the neighborhood. While those moms were getting old, mommy was staying young by skating in the street with us, riding bikes with us, even posing as a teenager attending summer day camp with us!! Mommy didn't work full time until I was in fourth grade, so she spent a lot of time volunteering at my school. The teachers treated me differently/better I feel because my mom was so involved.

A Mother's Heart

My mom was an LVN and worked through a registry per diem. She didn't get benefits, vacation or 401k, but she made good money. One day, my parents were having a discussion about that, and my dad bet her that she couldn't get a full-time job and earn a vacation. Of course, she responded that she could. She went out the next day and got one. She became employed at the phone company. Boy ole boy did she prove him wrong!! Mommy has remained employed for twenty-nine years and counting. Her work ethic is impeccable. She is the perfect example of hard work and dedication. She worked split shifts in the beginning. She would drop me off at school, go to work, pick me up, feed me and drop me off at home, and then head back to work.

Mommy taught me so much about life, instilling certain values and morals in me at an early age. She is always the "cup half full person," never negative and always willing to help. She also started working on building my self esteem early on. By me being a plus size girl, Mommy always made sure I was dressed appropriately and was comfortable with my height, weight and over-all look. She never let me walk around with my shoulders hunched and my head down. I was the best thing since sliced bread in my household, so when I was in the world nothing anyone said to me or about me even mattered because I was a SUPER STAR to my mother.

My mom told me everything that she knows about life, including finances, the importance of good credit, relationships, sex, employment, etc. If she knew it, she taught it. She was the best teacher not only to me and my brother, but to our friends as well. She would have reading sessions with us and the neighborhood kids sitting on the porch. We lived in Compton, so sometimes she would have the most treacherous gang bangers in "the hood" reading a book, asking how to pronounce a word and feeling that they could do or be something other than what they were at that time just because of the attention and concern for them that Mommy showed.

With all the things that Mommy taught and showed me, I still chose to grow up and do things my way. My mother never made me feel bad about the things that I did or the paths that I was choosing. She would always help me through it and re-educate me on her previous lessons. I never remember her telling me "I told you so" or throwing my mistakes in my face. She would never chastise me in front of others. Even if I was wrong, we maintained a united front when others were around. Behind closed doors she would tell me I was wrong and discipline me accordingly. Even when I was married, my husband would 'tell on me.' He used to say the reason I acted like that is because she thought everything I did or said was cute. It wasn't that at all, but she would never express her dislike for those things in front of him, but she would definitely let me know about myself when it was just her and me.

Mommy made everything an adventure growing up. We never had to be concerned about finances, living arrangements or any adult issues. We never knew that money was tight at times until we were young adults. We thought that spending a day at the beach or park with a picnic lunch was a treat, not knowing money was low. Getting in the car and riding down streets and learning directions and landmarks was fun, but those were probably the times when there wasn't a lot of money to do other things. We never even knew on some of our road trips that we were lost. Mommy was too cool to let that show. All we knew is we were spending quality time with Mommy.

Mommy has always been bad with paying bills on time. When I was younger, sometimes I would come home from school and the phone would be cut off. I would go to a neighbor's house and call her at work, and she would say "It's right here in my purse with a stamp on it. Let me go downstairs and pay it." When she would let our lights get cut off, she would make the best of it. We would have a candlelight dinner and a candlelight bath. It would be the best. But come on now, how many times is that going to be fun. It would have been different if we didn't have the money, but to have the money and not pay had just become to be too much for me. She showed me how to pay bills, make our doctor and dentist appointments, travel arrangements and passed the torch to me when I was about thirteen.

After a certain age, my brother and my father started doing their own thing freeing up both Mommy's and my time allowing us to spend more time together. We started being best friends. If you saw Mommy, you saw me. We did and still do everything together. We ride to work, church, the nail shop, and the grocery store and travel and live together. We are the best roommates anyone could ask for. We help each other and respect each other's privacy and feelings.

There is never a time that I can think of that I needed my mother and she was not there. Whether I was celebrating or mourning, she was there. When my daughter was born, Mommy was right there. When my daughter passed away, Mommy was right there. When my father died, Mommy was right there. When my husband died, needless to say, Mommy was right there. I recently had major surgery, and I didn't think it was possible, but the way she took care of me made me love her even more.

I tell her all the time that I wish I could share her with other people because I am so so so lucky to have her. She brightens my days in the best kind of ways just by hearing her voice or seeing her smile. It is so comforting to know that there is someone in this world that genuinely loves me, respects, supports and wants the best for me. I wish everyone was as lucky as I am, and I thank God that He chose someone so special to be my #1 fan and supporter, my teacher, my doctor, my counselor, my protector, my rainbow after the storm, my MOTHER.

Through it All, I'm Still Standing

The Diane Jackson Story
by
Dalejuan Jackson

A Mother's Heart

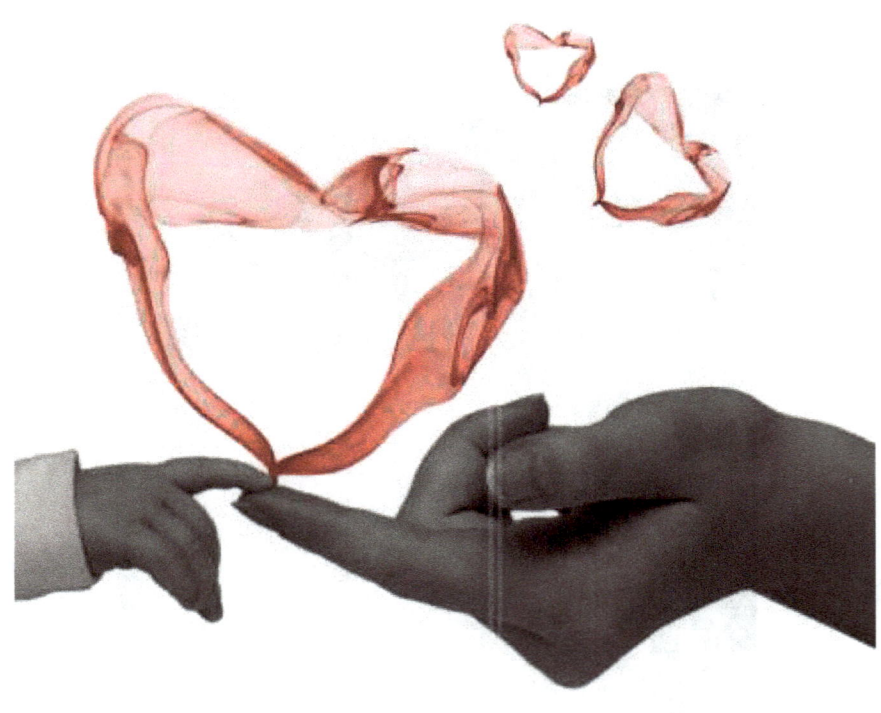

A Mother's Heart

My name is Dalejuan. I am seventeen years old. And I want to tell you how my life has been with my mother Diane Jackson for seventeen years. She is the greatest mother in the world to me. My mom and I have a very outstanding relationship.

In the beginning of 2004 was the first time I had ever experienced been scared. I almost lost my mother. She is the closest person to me. All I can remember is my sisters trying to hide something from me. My sisters were talking to each other, and I had heard crying and them saying Mama had been shot two times and she might not make it. I lay on the bed and cried. I also prayed myself to sleep, asking God, "Please don't let my mother die." My mother told and promised me when she got shot that she would leave the street life alone. It took my mom about five months to walk straight again. I never felt hurt like this before in my life. I thank God for my mom because she is still here today.

I learned how to pray and believe in God and have faith because my mom has always kept me in church as long as I can remember. Even when my mom was living the street life, she always made sure that I was in church every Sunday morning. I love my mom, and I am very thankful for her. No matter what she has done before in her life, my mama loves me and wants the very best for me. She raised me to be the nice young man that I am today. My father, whom I miss a lot, was a great father up to his death. My dad took very good care on me. Also, he made sure I had everything I needed and wanted. But, my mom taught me everything that I know. She is the one that keeps me dressed very nicely. My mother has always bought me nice clothes. During my whole life, my mom has always taken very good care of me.

My mom is the greatest gift I can ever have in my life. From the day I was born to present day, she has been by my side protecting me from the dangers of the earth. My mom Diane has given me the gift of life, and I want to dedicate this story to the greatest woman in my life.

During my childhood, my mom and I had the best of times as we did everything together, such as go to the park or go to watch a movie at the theatre. My mom is the greatest person in the world because she knows what to say and when to say it. When I was going through hard times, she was there to comfort me and say it was okay to feel that way and everything would be all right. My mom has been there through everything, such as a bloody nose to having a family member pass away in my life. She takes care of me every day and cares about me like no one else in the world can. She feeds me, gives me a place to live, and will love me no matter what happens on this earth.

The day I was born, my mom held me in her arms, and she has never let go since. She protects me from going in the wrong direction in life and keeps me grounded and moving forward. She helps me decide what's wrong from right and what is good for me and how I can improve every day. Diane is the best mom a son can have. She will go great lengths to protect her baby and do anything to keep me safe. She can be loving when I need her to, as well as being protective when it's needed. My mom is my best friend because I can tell her everything without being judged. She listens to me and gives me advice better than a therapist can do. She can turn the darkest days into a bright day in just minutes. She is my all, and I will do everything for her as well. I will also protect her from danger and do anything through the end of time.

My mom, Diane is also the greatest cook I know. She cooks anything that I can think of, and it is delicious. It is better than a restaurant or any of my other family members. She can be the world's greatest chef by a long slide. Diane is the best at everything. Cooking, working, and loving, she can do it all with ease. My mom can have a bad day or two and still have powerful words to say to make anyone's day brighter. Every day, she stays strong for people who count on her to be a great example. She is my hero because she stays strong and moves on from all the hardships she has to deal with in her life. She never shows what problems she has and keeps moving forward to better her life. She will always be my hero, my mom, and the best person in the world. Diane will stay strong and be in my heart until the end of time. No matter what happens, I will always love her and be there to guard her through any dangers or adversity. She has protected me throughout my life, and I will do the same for her no matter what it takes. My mom is my whole life, and I will do anything for her.

During my whole life, my mom Diane has done more for me than I can imagine. She has cared for me even though we have some arguments once in a while. Even though sometimes we don't connect on everything, we will always be best friends and love each other. Together, we make a perfect team, and we do everything together. That's why we are best friends.

My mom is the most beautiful woman on this earth. She is a goddess in her own right. She can shine light in the midst of the darkness. Diane can walk past someone and make him or her feel like a brand new person. She can talk to people and change their lives by giving them advice to better their lives. My mom gives advice to my family, and they come out better people. She is really a life changer and a good person inside and out. Diane is an angel that is alive on earth that has been sent from the heavens to protect and guide me. She is here to give me my own wings and send me on the right path in life. Everywhere she goes, she sets fireworks off and has a great smile to make everyone happy. My mom is better and greater than any celebrity or more beautiful than a rose. She will climb any mountain to see a better destination. Even if she is not rich in money, she is always rich with love, and she will spread the wealth to anyone who wants it.

My mom has the voice of an angel when she sings in the church with the choir. She is very is close to God. She loves God, and I know God loves her even more. She prays every night for a stronger and better day tomorrow, and God grants her wish. Diane is the heart and soul in my family, and she is truly a gift from God. My mom will be in my life way after she is gone from the earth, and I will never forget about what she has done for me. I will always have the greatest memories with her, and I will create more in the future as well.

She is not the most famous, but she is a star in my eyes. She shines brightly and leads the way to heaven. My mom is the apple of my eye and is the greatest mom a child can have. She will pick me up when I fall and clean me up when I'm dirty. My mom is the one I can count on to help with my ideas or protect me from harm. Diane will love me when I start my own family and when she will have more grandchildren. And when she does, she will love them the same way she loves me.

When I was young, my mom took me places to make memories and enjoy life together. We went to the beach where my mom and I built sandcastles and swam in the ocean. We dug holes in the sand and jumped in there as if we were trying to find treasures. Pretending we were pirates, we ran with fake swords and tried to talk funny. She also took me to watch plenty of movies at the theatre like *Finding Nemo, Peter Pan*, and more. We went almost every weekend, and we still go occasionally. We also did arts and crafts, like drawings or making birdhouses while reading kids stories together. We read many books written by Dr. Seuss, but my favorite is *Sam I Am*. We also read poems that were funny and exciting also written by Dr. Seuss.

During my first year of school, my mom was the first one I would count on to help me with my homework and my projects. When a problem was too hard or a project was too messy, my mom would come and help me out with no cost. She would participate in all of my fundraisers and go to all of my school events. My mom would do all she could to help me succeed in school, and she still does today. Without my mom, I don't know where I would be and what I would be doing today. My mom wants me to succeed in life because she has seen people go the wrong way in life, and she wants me to be a better person. Diane is the love of my life, and she means the world to me. I would do anything to protect her from any danger we come across in this world.

My mom is the best woman in the world simply because she gives without expecting anything back. She gives all she can to help people in the time of need, and she does it just because she knows that it is the right thing to do and because God has sent her on this earth to help people. She helps people because she knows it's hard for people, and she wants to do as much as she can. She gives great advice and amazing speeches to change people for the better. She also will listen to your problems and say what is needed and will not hold back. My mom will change a person's life in just five minutes.

Great parents love their children unconditionally, and that's what my mom does. Even if she doesn't know you, she won't judge you, but love you. She doesn't pick on all your flaws, but gives you pointers to improve. My mom loves anyone she comes across even if you don't do the same. She is kind hearted and is a blessing sent on earth. She can relate to you in many ways, and you can talk to her for hours about anything. My mom will amaze you in a thousand ways and entrance you with her knowledge. In my opinion, her heart might be the biggest one on this earth. She expects nothing, but she will give everything to you. My mom says that it is her mission on this earth to help people better their lives. Diane has been there for all who need a shoulder to cry on or an extra hand for help. She will always be pure and heavenly even through all the sins around her.

When you need a friend, my mom will be the best one. My mom is my best friend simply because she understands me like no one else can. She knows when I'm sad and need someone to talk to or when I'm tired and I need an extra blanket. She will be there to talk about what happened in school or help me with an extremely hard math problem. She knows what to do when I'm up late thinking about a past family member or where to go to calm me down when I need a rest. She is a goddess that will spread her wings to fly you to your destination or simply protect you from evil. Diane is a great mom as well as a great friend to have in my life.

Chasing her dreams is something she does constantly. Her dream is to have her son grow into a man, and she is doing a wonderful job. Her dream is to see me succeed as well as improve the world around her. She has affected my life greatly because she has guided me in the right direction. She has set my priorities straight and has made me a better man. She has given me the gift of life, and I want to give her the gift of love. I love her because she will love me back. Diane is a seed who has blossomed into a beautiful rose. She is still growing in knowledge and will keep growing just like I am. My mom is faithful and respectful in everything she does, and that's why everyone loves her.

All in all, I have witnessed an angel on this earth, and I know it is my mom. She has been sent down to guide me to my destination as well as help people through every single thing. My mom is indescribable, but I would like to come close to saying she is amazing.

Mommy

The Esperanza Jones Green Story
by
Quantanique S. Williams

Esperanza and Her Children

A Mother's Heart

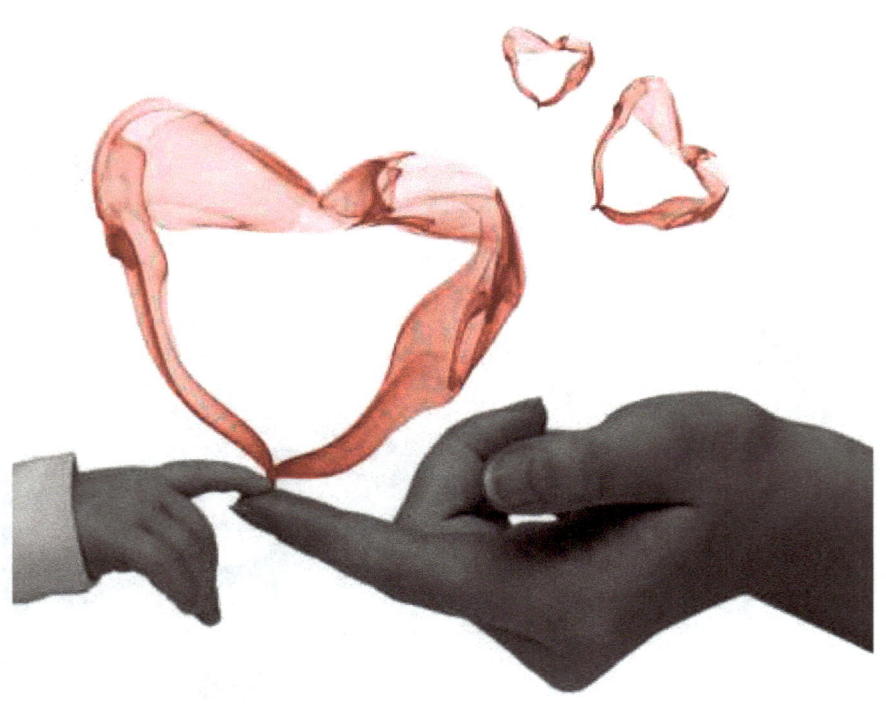

A Mother's Heart

My relationship with my mother is one that has grown in recent years, and her wisdom is something I need more than ever before as I'm now walking into motherhood. Just being pregnant and thinking of having to actually birth to this little person gives me a great respect for my mother for just deciding to bring me into this world at the young age of seventeen.

My mother has always been affectionate hugging, kissing and sharing her love through not just words, but actions, by always making sure my siblings and I were fed, well groomed and clothed.

What I admire most about my mother is her compassion for the less fortunate and the homeless. She is never ashamed to eat among them or give what she has to others. She serves in her community.

My mother taught me to never half do any task I take on whether it was a chore she told me to do, school work or a project I was working on. She taught us never to be racist and to embrace all others.

I love my mom's creativity. I remember always walking to Michael's Arts & Craft store with her when I was a young child. Now she beads and bakes all types of neat things.

Something I don't understand was why she didn't make visitation available to my father for three years when they were going through a divorce. Did she think of herself or did she have me and my sister Kierra in mind? I often wonder why she didn't have that one-on-one talk about puberty or what they call the bird-and-bees conversation with me. Did she feel uncomfortable? Did she not know how to because her mother was gone?

Something I'd like to do differently is actually have that conversation formally but casually with my child about his different stages in life, from the change of the body, to change of hormones, to the feeling of liking the opposite gender. I'd like to discuss clear expectations I have for him and instill the Lord in him at a young age. I'd like to be a woman who is content with being alone and that speaks up for herself and doesn't allow anyone male of female to talk to me any type of way. I dislike that my mother seems to do this and continues to stay, and I found myself in the same place years later.

My mother always encouraged my goals and supported my talents. I never felt ashamed of my artistic goals.

Esperanza Moreno Jones now Esperanza Moreno Green is my mother. I love her very much, and I'm thankful for her unconditional love and support.

The Love I Have for My Mother

The Vertie Mae McClinton Story
by
Millicent (McClinton) Redd

A Mother's Heart

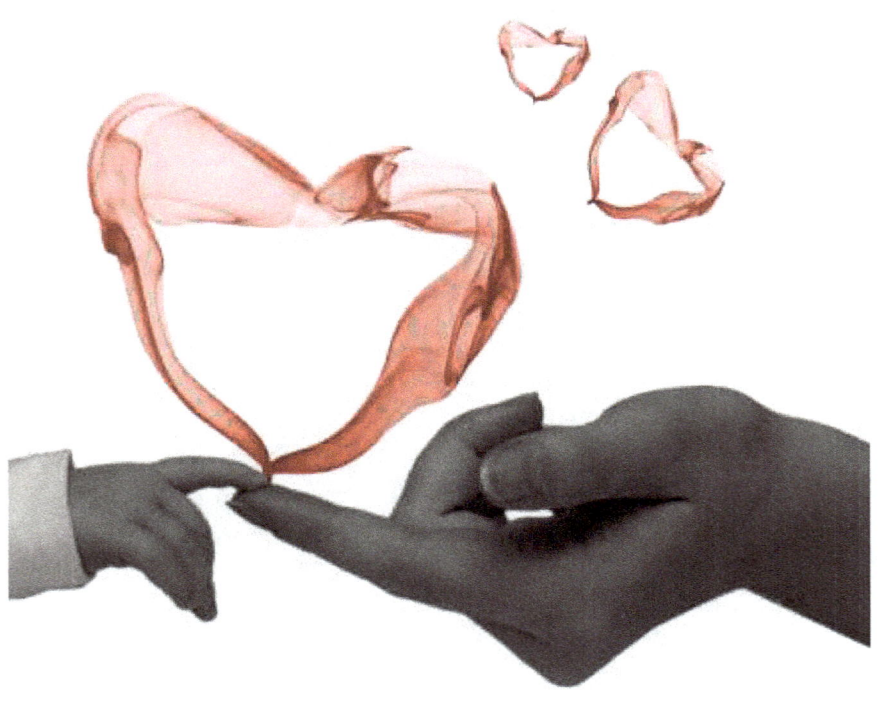

I am thanking God right now for my mother. She is still here with us today at seventy-two years of age, coming up to seventy-three in July 2013.

Some of my sweetest memories of my mother center on fragrances. Our home was fragrant too, as she aired the house regularly, scrubbed the interior with pine cleaners throughout the rooms. A frequent memory I treasure is of my mom hanging clothes on the line to absorb the outdoor freshness. I can see her stretching to reach the clotheslines, as wooden clothespins filled her apron pockets and a few clamped between her teeth.

But I think the best smell was Mom's cooking early in the morning before we would get up. I remember one morning she decided to make something new for breakfast. She was happy about her new dish. Momma made fried potatoes with chopped green onions and scrambled eggs that had onions and another veggie. When we came into the dining room to eat, we all looked! What in the world is that Momma made? Looking at her face, with a big smile on it, we all decided to eat what Momma had prepared. She was so happy. At the end of the day, that is what mattered.

My first impression of my mom is the unconditional love that she has for all of us, just like Jesus. There are five children total in our household. Jesus has the same love for us, never wanting us to go in the wrong direction or making unwise decisions. That is how my mom was, and today, she is still the same way. That reminds me of this song, "Jesus loves me, and this I know, for my mother shows me so."

Momma never considered it a sacrifice to stay home with us while we were small. I am sure having five children at home was quite a handful; however, she never complained. I think at times it must have been difficult, but she always made sure all our needs were met.

I can remember when I was in junior high school, and it was coming to graduation time and my sister and I wanted to look different from the other girls. So our mother decided to make our graduation clothes, and we were the best-looking girls there. Everyone was saying how good we looked, not knowing that our mother made our graduation outfits. Another fun memory while we were in high school is our classmates thought my mother was our older sister. We never told them otherwise. Our weekend family outings with our mother and father, who has gone home to be the Lord, included going to Knott's Berry Farm, playing baseball in the park and sometimes in the yard, hearing Momma telling Daddy not to throw the ball so hard at us because we're girls. Momma always looked out for us.

During my father's illness, almost every evening was spent with the sound of my mother's well-modulated voice reading or singing to my father. I remember her sitting by his bed next to the lamp while Dad lay there looking so peacefully. Mom's gentle seriousness, coupled with her genuine appreciation of Dad was awesome to see. I saw it every time Mom's mouth began to work in that special way of hers that always culminates in helpless laughter.

Now, it's our turn to look out for Momma. All we have now is Momma. My momma is one of my best friends even though we don't see eye to eye. I love her with all my heart. When she is not feeling well, I am praying for her, always asking the Lord to give her long life on this earth.

My mom and dad really loved the Lord with all their hearts. I thank the Lord for them. Back in 1978, they went to a church called Love, Peace and Happiness Church. On the next night, they invited me and my sisters and brother to go. Now my mom is a little up in age, so she really doesn't drive anymore. So, every Sunday morning, we ride together to the house of the Lord. This is the best gift of all- to see my mother in the house of the Lord. Thank you, Lord.

A Mother's Heart

A Mother Like None Other

The Mercer Yvonne McClinton Story
by
Ahleeyah Nichols

Mercer and Ahleeyah

A Mother's Heart

I love my mom, but I don't even know where to start to describe the love and way I feel about my mother. My mom is Mercer Yvonne McClinton, and she is the best mother I could ever have. My mom is loving, kind, gentle, caring, and many more words I can describe her with. My mom has been through many trials and tribulations during her life, and as a result, she is a very strong and humble woman.

My mother has always taught me to keep God first in my life. While growing up, we would go to Love, Peace, and Happiness Church every Sunday. She taught me to keep God first because we need Him in our lives, and with God, anything is possible. I was taught that God would always get me through any situation even if I thought it was impossible.

No one in all my eighteen years of living has nurtured and encouraged me more than my mom. There has never been anyone there who comforted me more than my mom or has been there for me through my early adult years like my mom. The value I owe my mom is incalculable, but my love and appreciation for my mother is the best gift I can give her each day. My mom is not perfect. I know her faults and weaknesses, but they seem so small to me because of her great and positive influence in my life. My mom has taught me well and pointed me in the right path for life, and that overshadows any of her imperfections.

My mom has had a direct influence on my life, and I always took what she said into consideration, even if I didn't agree. My mom has had an influence in my life, and because of her influences, she is the only person I go to when I have questions or just want to talk. Because I have lived with my mom, we have always had a close bond. Each day when I got in from school, we would just sit and talk and have many heart-to-heart conversations. My mom knows I love her with all my heart; I would do anything for my mother.

My mom and I have been through so much throughout my life. She has taught me to be a strong young lady. When my father passed away, my mom was there to comfort me each and every day. My mom would let me know each day would get easier. Sometimes, we would just sit and reminisce about all the wonderful times we had together as a family. After my dad passed away, my mom bought me a jewelry box that said "Love" on it and Bible scriptures that went along with love. I loved the fact that she gave me that gift because the scriptures helped me to cope with my loss. Inside the gift box, I put the flowers from my dad's casket as a keepsake.

I think since I'm genetically part of my mom, I automatically have some qualities just like her. Growing up watching my mom do things could have also had a powerful impression on me too. My mom likes many things, like reading, music and movies; I have those same likes, and I know they were passed on in my genes. My mom loves good music like Jazz, and she love Robin Thick and Eric

Benet. In my family, she is known for bumping Jazz music super loudly.

As her daughter, I have some type of musical talent; I have an ear for music, and I like everything loud no matter what I am listening to. My mom passed down a gift of writing to me, and both my mom and I are very good at it. She reads everything, like magazines, books, and newspapers, etc., and she writes plays.

Her life is like someone who found avenues for personal growth. My mom always thought and taught me there is room for improvement. She taught me how to take corrective criticism and told me it is good to be quiet. I appreciate everything my mom has done for our family. Raising two kids, washing, ironing, cleaning, and cooking isn't always an easy job when you're a single parent; it takes a lot of time and energy, but through it all, she still found time to read, which gave her peace and helped her to relax.

The thing that amazes me is through her busy schedule she still made time to read, whether it was a whole book or a single page. My mom took time in the day to nurture her inner self. She would read the Bible, and life for her was about her family; she didn't try to impress people; she just did her. Mom lived out the Bible passage about being content with what we had and didn't worry about what other people were doing. Competing for the valuable and visible items was not my mom's cup of tea.

A Mother's Heart

My mother represents unconditional love and care. Whenever I was having a dark, cloudy moment, I could always go to my mom for guidance. She has experienced more of the things that I go through or will go through in the future; my mom knows what to say to put me in a better mood. For me, my mother's words spell reassurance and security. My mom is someone who inspires and represents love, safety, trust, and concern. Even though we have our disagreements, we don't let that affect our mother-daughter relationship. I will always love my mom no matter what.

Her advice and actions that projects her love and concern for me always find their way into my heart and mind. Even though I try to ignore it, it seems like my mom's opinion is all I could think about. The love my mother gives is infinite, eminent and limitless. Her love for my brother and me lives on beyond a human's life span.

My mom is the best creation that God has made. She has many amazing powers, like being able to multitask without any complaints. She cares for everyone no matter what without any demands. All mothers are wonderful in their own way. My mom is very special because she carried two children and can carry hardships, but she holds happiness, joy, and love. She smiles even though she might want to scream. My mom sings when she might want to cry. She cries when she's happy and laughs when she's nervous. My mom fights for what she believes in and does not take no for an answer when there is a way to solve the problem. My mom goes without, so her children can have. My mom loves unconditionally, and I love her just as much. She cries when her children excel and cheers really loudly when we get awards and make her proud. My mom is strong, and there is no other strength like hers. Her hugs and kisses can heal a broken heart. There are many wonderful moms that come in all different shapes, sizes, and colors, but no other mother can compare to mine! My mom did more than just give birth to me and my brother; she gave us joy, hope, and love.

I thank God for my mom, Mercer McClinton; she has taught me many things throughout the years. My mom is a wonderful woman, and I am proud to say I'm her daughter. My mom has taught me the importance of having a relationship with God and with Him anything is possible. There isn't anything more important for a mother to teach her children than to teach them how to have a relationship with God. Mom taught me how to endure and to never give up, even if I am having a hard time. Growing up, we endured some hard times, but through my mom's example of endurance, we learned to keep going, even in the hard times.

My mom never complains; she just learned to endure. If we will obey God and endure hardship like a good soldier (2 Timothy 2:3), there will be ample reward. My mom has taught my brother and me to be faithful to our words and to be faithful to God and His Word. My mom taught me the difference between right and wrong and taught me to make proper decisions.

I am here today as a result of my mother's faith. She believed that by teaching me all that she taught, she would never have to shed tears over a disobedient daughter. No, I haven't done everything right. Yes, I've messed up at times, and I've done some things in the past that I shouldn't have done. But God is forgiving, and the words of my mom always came to me in my time of need. God has been faithful to answer the prayers we prayed over the years.

Out of all the women and mothers in the world, there is no other that could take the place of my mom. Even though we get on each other's nerves at times, we still have unconditional love for one another. I know my mom loves me and cares for me. My mom loves me enough to ask where I'm going and what and with whom; she loves me enough to try and tell me to save my money for a rainy day; that's great because all children don't have parents that care for them the way mine cares for me.

There are so many things that I want to say to you Mom, I decided to put it in writing. In this story Mom, I want to share with you how I feel about all of the wonderful things that you have brought into my life. I want you to know how you have influenced my life and how you molded me and shaped me to be the woman I am now. You deserve to be honored; you deserve to be thanked.

When you became a mother, not once, but twice, you chose a life of selflessness. You chose a life of dedication, giving and caring. You chose to give up a life as an independent woman in exchange for a life of nurturing your kids. You made a decision that you have held strong to for a lifetime. You chose to give up all selfish thoughts and desires that we humans have in exchange for loving, caring and doing for both of your children. God blessed you with two wonderful children, a boy and a beautiful girl. You had a need inside of you to care for us and do for us unlike any mother I have ever seen. I know that I haven't always understood your point of view or agreed with all of your decisions. In some cases, I've probably been mad at you. It took me some time to get it. I had to be a woman I suppose, before I really understood, because as I child we just do not have the knowledge to comprehend the devotion and the commitment that mothers offer. I really appreciate everything you have done for me, and I am glad that you're my mom.

You could have chosen to be childless. You could have chosen a career and status. You could have chosen so many things for your path in life, but you chose us; you chose one boy, one girl and a bad dog we call Oreo. I want to thank you for being my mom and thank you for choosing me instead of something or someone else.

A mother does so many things for her child during a life's

time. It would be utterly impossible to list them all. I can share things with you that I can share with no other. I don't have to worry about the repercussions. I don't have to worry about being judged. I just share with you my fears, my thoughts, my hopes and my dreams. I can share with you anything and everything that I have a need to share. When I'm feeling somewhat inadequate, you are right there to encourage me. You reassure me that there is nothing I can't do. You believed in me when I didn't even believe in myself. You gave me strength and courage. You taught me not to let fear of a challenge or fear of the unknown keep me from going after my dreams.

For a woman to have so little of the finer things in life and to do what you have done for others for an entire lifetime is commendable. No, you are not Mother Teresa, as the world knows her, but you are my Mother Teresa. You have done for your children and your grandchildren without hesitation, over and over again, for your entire life. I don't think you will ever get the appreciation and gratitude that you so deserve. You have repeatedly done without things that you need or desire in order to give what you have to your children. You have given way more than should ever be expected from one person.

I wonder if others are aware, as I am, of everything you've done for them. I know that if I needed a dollar you would hand it to me. You would give me your last dollar without any hesitation, without a question about why I might need it or how I was going to use it. You would just give to me your very last dollar. My mother's love is unconditional, and I love my mom unconditionally no matter what.

I am who I am because of you. I love you, and I thank you for everything you have done for me. I thank you for teaching me all that you can; I thank you for being there for me and raising me the best way you know how. I am very proud to say you are my mom, and I'd yell it to the entire world. Thank you, Mom, for just being you! I respect you and admire you. I am proud to be your daughter.

I've never known anyone in my life as giving as you. I look up to you, I appreciate you, and I am grateful for you. I accept you for who you are and who you are not. It makes me happy when I can do for you. I love you very very much, and I thank you for everything you have done for me and my brother. You are the best mom, and I wish everyone else could have a mom as great as you are.

A Mother's Heart

A Mother's Heart

Mom- Gentle Strength

The Mildred Mae (Dunlap) Williams Story
by
Julia Lary

The Williams' Family Matriarch

A Mother's Heart

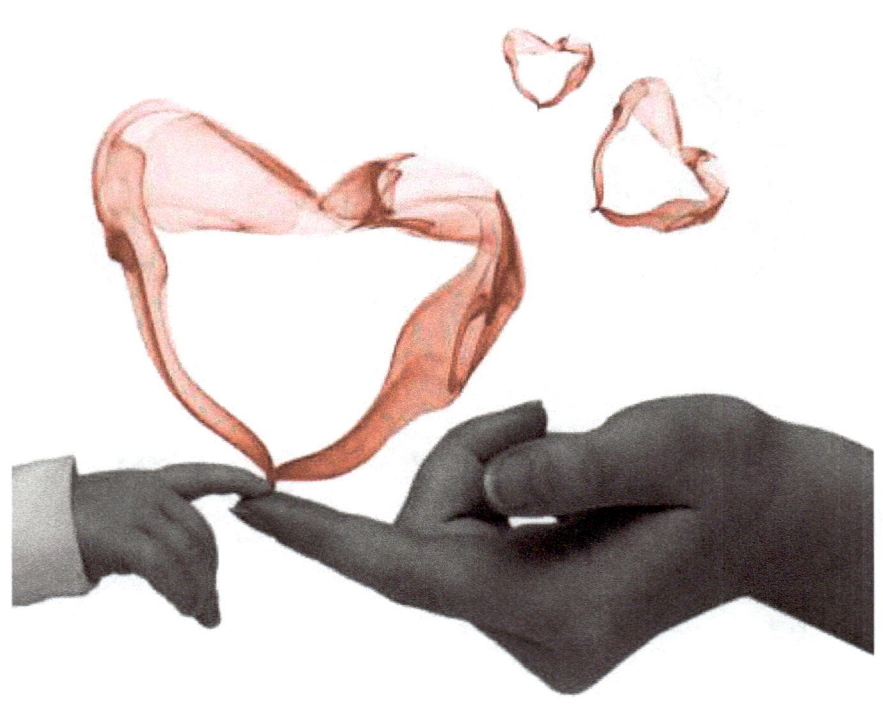

When you become of age, it's hard to look back on your life as a child. When I was about eleven years old, my dad left us to go to another city to find work in order to care for his family. My mom told us Dad would not be coming back until the weekend. Since there were many of us sharing a bed, I asked if I could sleep with her and the baby until his return. She said, "Yes."

I don't remember how many weeks or months Dad had been gone before the baby passed away, but I do know that I felt maybe I had gotten on the baby some way, somehow and killed her. My mom tried to convince me it was not my fault, but I felt Dad would say, "If you had not been in the bed with her, she would still be alive."

My mom showed me the doctor's report which read "SIDS." Did I know what that meant? Definitely not! SIDS is Sudden Infant Death Syndrome. Then, my mom said my baby sister didn't die because of me. She died of natural causes. Of course I asked when had she become sick, and Mom explained that we can sometimes get sick during the night, even as a healthy person, but no one will know what happened until the autopsy is complete. She told me she did not have to be sick to die. Later in life, I learned SIDS is also called "crib death." Bottom line, Dad didn't blame me, but seeing wreaths on doors afterwards always brought back the memories.

My dad's visits went from weekends to once a month to sporadic and finally not at all. Thankfully, there were friends and family members who were willing to help out because when the visits stopped so did the money for bills, etc. The only problem with this story was that the friends and family members who were willing to help didn't offer to give Mom money or food; they named a specific child from the family that they would take and care for. I didn't understand why we needed to leave home in order to receive help, but because of my mom's need for help, she agreed. I went to live with my dad's sister who wanted kids but was not able to have her own. The fifth child went to live with a church member, and the seventh child went to live with friends of the landlords who also had no children of their own.

Did I mention I was the second oldest of nine children? There were seven children when Dad left to go find work and by the time he decided to never return, there were nine. With that in mind, Mom still had to take care of six children. She became a welfare recipient but still needed to find work. She began working in a chicken house where chickens where prepared (killed and de-feathered, etc.) before making their way to the markets. She also worked for the "elite" cleaning house, preparing meals, laundry and whatever else needed to be done. There were also members of the "elite" who would let her pick up laundry, bring it home, wash and iron and deliver it back as a part-time job.

My mother was a strong woman, and one who never seemed to get tired, though I knew she did. On a side note, before I left home, I was the mother of all the other children, who had to make sure everyone was up in the mornings, dressed and ready for school, and we all had chores to do after school.

Mom was a sincere teacher of whatever she knew, and it appeared that since there was no dad in the home throughout most of our lives, she had the responsibility of teaching us everything. After having worked for a few years and realizing how hard it was to make ends meet, she instilled in us the value of work and working; that it was a requirement as well as a privilege, and we are to put all we have into any job we take on if we ever plan to succeed in life.

There were a couple of things she taught us that I've lived by each day of my life... 1) for every dollar you make always save a dime, and 2) never leave home without a wooden nickel (.05) for a phone call should an emergency arise. My mom taught us to never fall short of learning, always take the time to learn some things for ourselves because everything is not taught in classrooms, and it was not possible for her to remember everything we needed to know. She also stated that some of life experiences may never come up while we're home or still children, but as adults, we could still come to her and she would try to help find the answer. She used to say there were so many things of this world she could never teach us or help us with, but God can .... just ask Him. If you don't know what something means or how to perform a certain task, seek help. No question is a dumb question if you don't have the answer. If you don't know how to apply for credit or a job, ask someone who knows, read a book, or ask for wisdom from God. God can teach you all you need to know. I'm just a tool God uses to get you started. The rest is up to you and God.

Mom lived a life of brokenness for many years due to my father's separation from the family. I always knew that when she started talking about anger and prayer, she was either missing my dad or remembering how he left the family. I never knew the name of the song she'd always sing, but there's one verse I'll never forget ... "happy am I when all the dark clouds roll away." She would also continually repeat the 23rd Psalms, which is how I learned the passage.

(The Lord is my shepherd; I shall not want. He maketh me to lie down in green pastures; He leadeth me beside the still waters, He restoreth my soul; He leadeth me in the paths of righteousness for his name's sake. Yea, though I walk through the valley of the shadow of death, I will fear no evil; for thou art with me; Thy rod and thy staff they comfort me. Thou preparest a table before me in the presence of mine enemies; Thou anointest my head with oil; my cup runneth over, surely goodness and mercy

shall follow me all the days of my life; and I will dwell in the house of the Lord forever).

I didn't understand what it meant, but in church as a teenager, I was happy to announce that I knew the 23rd Psalms when asked if anyone could recite it verbatim. Before my dad left the family, we would always pray the Lord's Prayer when we were told to pray because in our early training to pray, that is what we were taught by our parents and the teaching of the church. In later years, Mom told us the bible says, "Ask and it shall be given to you," meaning when you pray, ask for whatever it is that you're in need of, and He will give it to you. At that moment, she explained that prayer to the Lord can be done in other ways, such as talking to God just as we talk to her. Mom said prayer is the channel by which we receive our blessings.

Other times, I knew Mom was still dealing with her brokenness when she began to teach us about forgiveness. Forgiveness frees both parties involved. Mom stressed to us that we will have broken hearts even among us siblings, so it's very important that she teach us forgiveness. She indicated that once we become adults and have our own children, it is important to teach them God's word, teach them to read the bible every chance they get, and most importantly, we must teach our children how to forgive as well. If our children are ever exposed to our anger, make sure they're around when we show grace. They must know that God's grace is sufficient for all... His mercy is new every morning. She said, "I am telling you this because I want you to learn from the mistakes of your parents, so that you won't have to go through the same thing I did and pass it on to your children." She added, "The bible says in Ephesians 4: 26... do not let the sun go down while you're still angry, and do not give the devil a foothold." That means, forgive when you are hurt and don't take your resentments/anger to bed. Forgiveness positions you where God can bless you.

My mom was an excellent soprano singer. We were taught to sing by my parents who could sing well in my opinion. We were raised in the church and thus have attended church all our lives. As a song leader in the church, my mom and dad would teach us songs on Saturdays that they were planning to sing on Sunday. Although we did not own a piano, my parents learned music the old fashioned way, through Solfege or as some know it ... solfa syllables (do, re, mi, fa, sol, la, ti, do). My first solo was taught to me at age ten by my mom ... "How Firm a Foundation." Here are the words to the beautiful song loved by my mom:

> "How firm a foundation, ye saints of the Lord, is laid for your faith in His excellent word! What more can He say than to you He hath said, to you who for refuge to Jesus have fled,

Fear not, I am with thee; O be not dismayed, For I am thy God, and will still give thee aid; I'll strengthen thee, help thee, and cause thee to stand, upheld by My righteous, omnipotent hand.

When through the deep waters I call thee to go, the rivers of woe shall not thee overflow; For I will be with thee thy troubles to bless, and sanctify to thee thy deepest distress.

When through fiery trials thy pathways shall lie, My grace, all sufficient, shall be thy supply; The flame shall not hurt thee; I only design thy dross to consume and thy gold to refine.

The soul that on Jesus still leans for repose, I will not, I will not desert to his foes; that soul, though all hell should endeavor to shake, I'll never, no never, no never forsake!"

After many years of singing the song, I really didn't understand what it meant or what my mom was trying to say when she taught the song to me, except I felt she was still dealing with her brokenness. I believe now, God was saying to her... "*Fear not, for I have redeemed you, I have summoned you by name, you are mine. When you pass through the waters, I will be with you; and when you pass through the rivers, they will not sweep over you. When you walk through the fire, you will not be burned; the flames will*

A Mother's Heart

not set you ablaze. I am the Lord, your God, the Holy One of Israel, your Savior" (Isaiah 43: 1-3).

Even though my mom only finished ninth grade, she was very cognizant. She was a brilliant learner in her efforts to improve herself. She was not afraid to tackle any task no matter how large or small. Mom read the Bible frequently and knew as much as anyone I've known of its contents. As adults, we teased her about not being afraid to jump in with the "well to do" church goers, and she would say, "My bible tells me no one is more than I am, that we are all equal in God's eyes, but I'm to put others before me in that I'm not to be selfish as in thinking of myself first." (Paraphrased)

I admired my mom for her tenacity. She was strong willed and the most giving person I've known. She was full of love; with nine children, she definitely had enough to share. She loved us all equally, and regardless of our faults, she always tried to direct us down the right path as much as she was able, and as she would say, "I'll leave the rest to God." The thing I'd hoped would be different after a few years was to see my mom and dad reunited before we became adults. At fifteen years of age, I had my own car and visited my mom and siblings often.

As young adults, my siblings and I showed our appreciation to Mom by helping her as much as possible, by purchasing TVs, small appliances, clothing or whatever she needed up to and including a car. She was a one-of-a-kind mom who went to be with Jesus in 1996, on Easter Sunday. What a wonderful celebration it was with all the children there. God blessed her with a good life before her departure. Her love still shines in all of us today. Even the grandkids who knew her speak of the legacy of love she left behind.

A Mother's Heart

A Mother's Love

The Katherine (Williams) Heath Story
by
Tundra (Heath) Alfred

A Mother's Heart

A Mother's Heart

I have the honor of writing about my mother Mrs. Katherine Williams-Heath. My mother was born in Pine Bluff, Arkansas and is the daughter of the late Walter and Mildred Williams. My mother was a straight "A" student and dancer with a love for writing and singing. She is married to Mr. Dwight Heath and is the mother of two children.

She is a caring, loving, and devoted wife and mother. My words can never express the love I have for her. As I grew up, she was always there for my brother and me. I could not imagine life without my mother. My mother's love reminds me of the love that Jesus has for us: forever unconditional. That is a love that we should all want to strive to have. I hope and pray that my children will see my love for them in this way! When you look up the word mother, friend, wife, loving and virtuous in the dictionary, you will find my mother.

There are many things I could tell you about my mother, but I will just share a few. As a child, I dreamed of a wonderful mother-daughter relationship. Well, while I knew my mother loved me and she would always be there for me, I did not feel like we had that special bond that other mothers and daughters have. My mother has always been a very soft spoken woman. She never has unkind words to say to or about anyone. Mom always pushed us to strive to be the best. I think if she has a gray hair on her head, it came from me. I won't say I was the rebellious child but between my brother and me, I was all over the place.

Mom cut no slack when it came to school! I went through things in high school that your average teenage girl goes through, and Mom was always there. Then, something happened that would in my mind strain the relationship between my mother and me forever. My parents divorced, and I felt my life was over! Never in a million years did I think that would happen. I never once saw my parents fight. Then, my mother left just when I needed her the most. Mom was still there to love me and talk to me, and I even went and spent weekends with her. Then came the day I went to live with her. I just knew this was going to be the start to a new relationship with my mom!

Well, Mom was still Mom, soft spoken but stern! She allowed me to be me and learn from my mistakes. My mother did not have to command respect from her children; it just came naturally! I decided to join the service. Mom, I think was a bit shocked, but she was there with me every step of the way! After leaving for the service, I began to be home sick and encountered problems that I had never faced in life. I would call home and my mom would be so supportive, caring, understanding and loving. She was my war buddy. In my own mental and physical war, she was in the trenches with me.

I knew my mother was a strong woman, but I just never really understood. I saw my mother in a new light! She never let me give up; she always had positive and encouraging words to say to me. Although I knew some things were probably tearing her apart, she was being strong for me so that I could finish what I had started! During these times, my mother was not only my mother, but she became my best friend. You see, God has a way of giving us and showing us just who we need and when we need them. I called my mom every chance I got while in training just to talk. She has never told me, "I told you so" or "Baby, just give up." Her words even to this day are, "You stand tall and always do your best, and when it becomes too much to bear, give it to God!" Wherever my travels took me, I wanted my mother to be right there. While she could not be there physically, she was always with me in spirit!

I always prayed my parents would get back together (every divorced child's hope and dream). Well, while I was stationed in Korea, I called home to hear my mother answer the phone. To my surprise, she told me that she and my father had gotten back together. I began to cry. All I remember saying was, "God answered my prayers!" Then, I asked why she never told me in the midst of our conversations, and she replied, "I did not want to get your hopes up." Wow! Again a mother's love continuing to think of how her children might feel in a situation that might not work out!

My mother is the back bone and strength of our family. Her love for God is truly an example to live by. My mother has been there for us through dating, marriage and having our children. My mother is now a grandmother. She has three grandsons with another on the way and one granddaughter all of whom she has been there for their births. (Aren't we special!) My mother rarely tells us no! I live out of state and on every occasion that I have needed her to be here, she has packed her bags and come. I was working on my bachelor's degree while pregnant with my daughter. My mother was here for her birth, and I was in the middle of doing my paper for graduation.

My mom told me, "Baby, you need to rest. You just had a baby. Your professors understand (which they did), but I was determined to get all my work done. My mom made sure that I got rest and ate. She assisted with my daughter when needed. I know I stressed her out and even hurt her feelings at one point. I did not do it intentionally, but my mother was still the trooper and helped me to finish my paper by proofreading and ensuring that all my I's were dotted and my T's were crossed. Outside of having my children, that was probably the first time my mother saw me as a wife, mother and student all at the same time and full of determination to make sure that everything was done and in order. The look on her face when it was all done let me know that she was so very proud of me.

My mother and I can talk about anything. While I still miss the bond of being able to have mother-daughter time or being able to take pictures of my mother, daughter and myself, what I do know is that the bond that we now share is more than a picture or a lunch date. When my daughter was born, I wanted to name her after my mother. My mother said no it was too old-fashioned, so my daughter's name is derived from my mother's name, and they both share the nickname Kate. It was my way of showing my mother that her life and love mean so much to me.

My mother has a special bond with all her grandchildren. She has been a mother figure to the oldest and his love for her is like a son would have for his mother. She is our matriarch, the eyes to our past and our hope for the future. There is no better love than that of a mother or a grandmother. I thank God for allowing us to still have her to share in the joys of life and to help us to instill morals and values in the lives of our children. What I have learned from my mother can never be replaced or taken away.

She has taught me the value of life, to love God with all my heart, how to be a respectful and virtuous woman, wife, sister and mother, to be the best and never give up, but most of all to love myself beyond measure. My mom is a very private person, so I do not think I have ever asked her what her dreams, goals or ambitions were when she was a child, I can only begin to imagine as she loves to read and write. She never asks for anything and is always thinking of what we need or would like to have.

Every day is mother's day when it comes to my mother. Mom has written numerous poems and greeting cards; some of which have been published. How do you thank someone who has given you life and loves you unconditionally? You cherish every moment you have with them, tell them you love them, do what you can for them without them having to ask, and strive to make them proud!

I can only imagine that my brother and I have made my mother proud that there are no unsettled moments in her heart that we may have caused. To this day, I call my mother just to say I love you and make sure she is okay because I never want a day to go by that I do not say I love you! She never misses a birthday or a moment just to say 'I love you' or I just called because I was thinking of you. Mom never takes her eyes off God. Her faith and relationship with God is one that I strive to emulate. She encourages all of us to have a closer walk and relationship with God, and I know that because of her and my desire to have an intimate relationship with God is why my children have such a great desire and love for the Lord.

I know that my mother's strength and humbleness come from her mother and the way she was raised. Her relationship with her mother was one of love and respect. I never saw or heard my mother talk back or disrespect her mother. Their relationship was close. They were friends, and they shared a lot of things together.

She is a wife of unconditional love. When I see her in the role of a wife, she never oversteps her bounds as a wife. She is supportive, encouraging, loving and ever giving of herself. She is a true example of a woman whose husband is the head of the home.

Please do not get it twisted. She is not run over or disempowered by any since of the matter. My father understands and respects the role she has as a wife and a mother. It takes a strong woman and humbled woman to truly understand her honored role as a wife and mother, and my mother handles it graciously. I thank God for giving me to the earthly mother that He did. He knew that she would be the woman who would help bring me through the storms that I would face and keep me focused on Him.

So on this day, I just want to say to my mother, "Thank you for your unconditional love, for following your heart and giving us life, continued support, being a virtuous woman of God, a role model for me as a wife, mother, sister and friend and for instilling in us the morals, values and respect to get us through life. I know the role of a mother is not easy but you never gave up on us or the vision that God gave you about our lives and our children. I pray that God will continue to show us all favor and allow you to be here to see your grandchildren grow to fulfill the vision that God gave you for each of them."

A Mother's Heart

My Mom

The Tundra (Heath) Alfred Story
by
Micaiah Alfred (Age 9)

A Mother's Heart

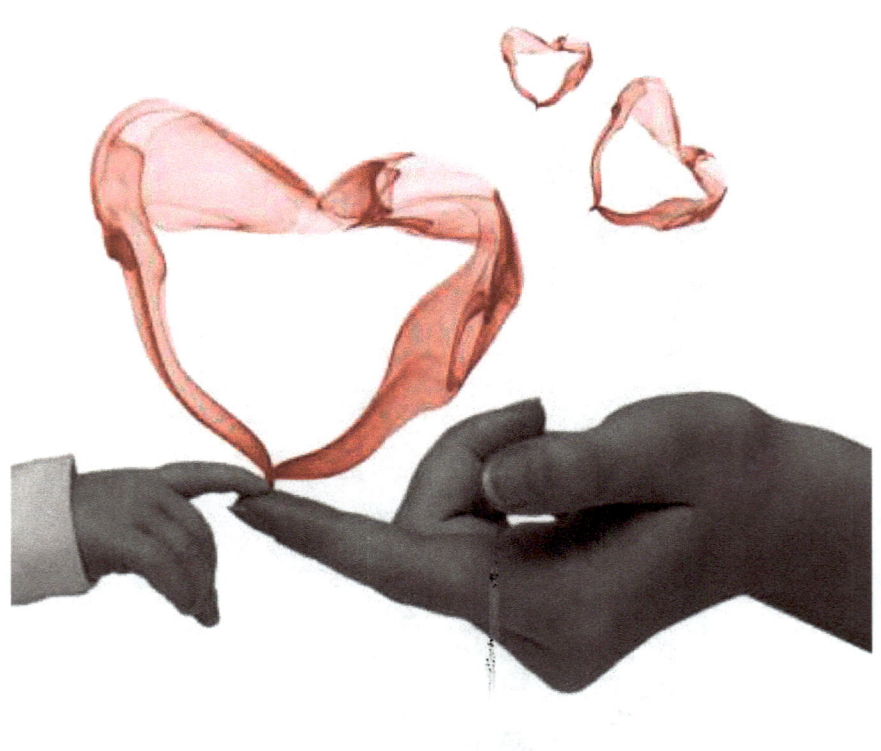

A Mother's Heart

My mom is a wonderful person. Her name is Tundra Alfred; we live in Baton Rouge, Louisiana. My mom was born in California, to my grandparents Mr. Dwight and Katherine Heath. My mom is married to my father Casey Alfred, Sr. God could not have blessed me with a better mother. My mom takes very good care of me and my sister Kaitlyn.

When I think of my mom, she makes me smile. She tells my sister and me stories and reads the bible to us. My mom makes us laugh, is there when we are sick, makes sure we have clothes and food to eat, attends all of our school and extracurricular activities, and, most of all, loves us unconditionally. I remember when my mom worked a regular job; we had to get up extra early to ensure everyone was where they needed to be on time.

Now, my mom owns her own home-based Travel Agency, is really great at being a small business owner and travel agent and is available for us all the time, and we do not have to get up extra early. She is a great wife to my dad as well; she makes sure that everything runs smoothly while he is away at work. It can get pretty hard sometimes, but she always tells us with God all things are possible.

My mom can be pretty strict sometimes and get really upset if we do something wrong. Then, she finds a way to relate it to a scripture in the Bible and tells us how our decisions will and can affect us later in life. When things go wrong in school, she is always there to help me fix it and do better. My mom is currently homeschooling my little sister until she can start Pre-K! I have watched my little sister grow and learn things pretty quickly!

My mom stresses the importance of learning and working for what we want, so when we do well in school, complete our chores and do things without asking, she does not let them go unrewarded. But if we do not do what we are supposed to, she deducts our rewards. What I like most is that my mom is teaching us to be respectful, loving and caring Christians. This is not always easy, but we try to do the right thing. Mom always stresses the importance of family and that we need to stick together and always pray for each other.

Mom really tries to keep us from listening to so much rap music and influences us by listening to Gospel and Praise and Worship, as well as classical music. My mom shows us on TV the kids and people that don't have homes and tells us we should appreciate the things that we have that other people do not have. We are looking forward to being able to perform community service now that Kaitlyn is older.

I am so proud of my mom. I learned that my mom attended college full time while she was pregnant with me and made excellent grades. She then returned to college in 2007 to obtain her Bachelor's Degree. She had my sister in December of 2008 and graduated Cum Lade in March of 2009 with her Bachelor of Science in Human Services. Mom is now praying that God will bless her to be able to go back to school to obtain her Master's in Human Services.

Watching my mom live her life and often times putting her goals on hold to ensure that we obtain our goals in order to be good children is inspiring. It makes me realize how much she really loves us. I am also learning how to be an entrepreneur as I often help my mom with her business by setting up for events and passing out business cards and flyers.

My mom is one of my favorite cooks. I love when she makes me gumbo, pinto beans and rice, spaghetti, jambalaya, mac and cheese, chili dogs, and shrimp etouffee. I enjoy learning how to cook with my mom; she has shown me how to cook cornbread from scratch and homemade pizza. I could not be a happier young man. My mom is one of my best friends, and I enjoy the quality time we spend together. My mom has taught me how to knit hats, be disciplined, follow through with things that I start, and always be a leader and not a follower.

I still have a lot to learn in life, but I know that with my mom and God's help, I will be the best in all that I do. I have learned that my mom is a very faithful friend and that those that she considers to be friends really value her friendship, trust and respect her. She is a leader in the church and a deacon's wife. I am not sure what that means, but I am still learning. As you can see my mom is the best mom that I will ever have.

I love you, Mommy!

A Mother's Undying Love

The Gloria L. (Williams) Harrison Story
by
Dr. Cassundra White-Elliott

Gloria and Cassundra

A Mother's Heart

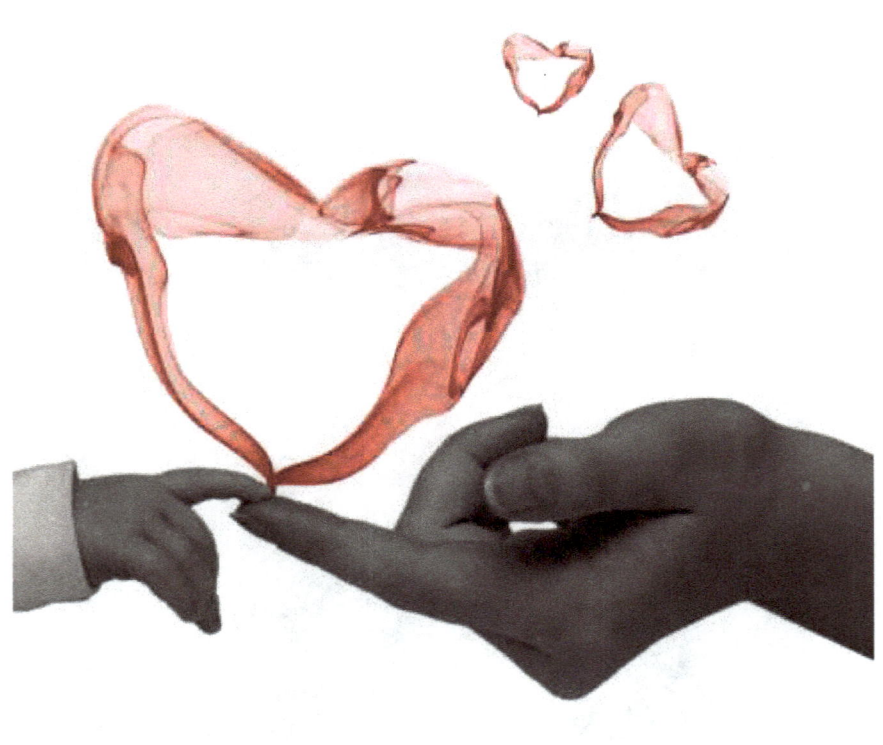

MOTHER

A creation with a heart of gold,
With the instinct to love and to hold,
A being of humanity with the devotion to care,
No matter what... she was always there.

Mother divine and elegant,
Special in her own way.
Appreciate what she does,
We cheer... hip-hip hooray.

Losing her was tragic and painful.
But, we know where she'll go.
Remembering the love somewhat eases the pain,
Life without her will never be the same.

We press on with a lot of pride; Mom would want us to,
Even though the pain we cannot hide.
Joy of memories of years gone by,
Still, hold your head up high,
For one of her accomplishments, we're the reason why...

PoeticArk,
Noah A, Williams, Sr.

Momma

Momma... It's more than just a word to me.
It doesn't just refer to my mother.
It's more than a parent, more than a 'caregiver,' more than a friend.
Someone that's there through thick and thin, to the very end.
Her love can't be replaced.
Her presence can't be erased.
There is a piece of her heart that is with me, my siblings, her grandchildren, and great-grandchildren.
The full meaning, the feeling, the emptiness, can be hard to comprehend.
She is still here with us, but it's not the same.
No one else can take that name.
I love my Momma... I miss my Momma.

August S. Harrison

At the tender age of sixteen, Gloria Louise (Williams) Flemister gave birth to her second child and only daughter: me, Cassundra Lynett Flemister (White-Elliott).

As a child and as an adult, I always felt the love of my mother. I never once had to wonder if she loved me. I could tell by everything she did for my brothers and me that she would do anything in her power to protect us from harm and to make sure our every need was met, and she did.

When I was three years of age, my mother moved my brothers and me to Los Angeles, California from Pine Bluff, Arkansas. She left my father, her husband, behind because of his abusive tendencies. At that point, she began to raise us as a divorced, single parent until she remarried a few years later, at which time, she gave birth to her fourth and final child. At the time of our arrival in California, she was only nineteen years old, but she was very independent. Of course, she had her mother, who did not live too far, to assist her with anything she needed.

When I was four years old, my brother and I began our schooling. My brother went to kindergarten, and I began pre-kindergarten, as we are only one year and one month apart in age. I was excited to begin school, and from that point on, my educational adventures began.

As I continued throughout the elementary years of my education, I remember coming home from school many days to find books lying on my bed. When I was young, my

A Mother's Heart

mother purchased various Scholastic books for me. At school, ever so often, the students would receive Scholastic Book order forms. Upon receipt of my form, I would always circle the books I wanted to purchase, after having read their descriptions. Perhaps, my mother saw my list and ordered my books. I too bought many of my books with the small amounts of money I saved. Because my mother was a single parent, my brothers and I did not bother her with asking her for this and for that. We always tried to be of help rather than little hindrances. We love our mother dearly, and we did not want to add to any struggles that she may have had.

As I grew older, the books my mother purchased for me would usually be part of a series; most of them were mysteries and detective novels. When I finished a book in the series, my mother would buy me one or two more. As an adult, not too long ago, I reflected upon this memory, and I asked my mother why she always purchased books for me, especially when I did not specifically ask for them. Her response was, "I always knew you loved to read. You always read everything, everywhere we went." Her heartfelt answer, though simple, touched my heart because it let me know that she knew my innermost desires, even when I was a child. Also, her comment told me something about myself that I did not know. Let me clarify my statement. Of course, I know that I have always loved to read, but I did not know (or remember) that as a child I went around reading everything I saw.

To me, that single action of her knowing my desires is demonstrative of a caring mother. When a mother takes time to know her child, it is because she cares for the child.

For a period of time, my mother stopped buying me books for my leisure reading, for I had grown older and had gone to college. At that time in my life, I had to buy books for college and needed to focus on my studies. However, after obtaining a degree or two and after watching a television commercial advertising a newly released book, I began to read books by my now-favorite author: Mary Higgins Clark- a suspense novelist. Clark puts out one book a year. Each year, I would wait in anticipation for her new novel. I talked to my mother about these books so much that she began to buy them for me. This again touched my heart.

Her actions told me again she loved me and what is important to me is important to her. She was aware that as an adult with a lucrative career, I could buy my own books. But, it was never about money. It was the personal satisfaction one gets when he/she fills the desire of another. I know it made her feel good to make me feel good and loved. And I made sure she knew that I appreciated the time she took to go to the store to buy my book or to order it online and the money she spent doing so. To me, that is an example of the special things mothers do for their children, when the children least expect it.

Not only did my mother know I had a love for reading as a child, but she also knew that I had a love to teach and to write. At the end of each year of elementary school, the teachers would clear out extraneous papers, worksheets, old books, etc. As they would begin to toss the papers in the trash, I became horrified. I could not understand why someone would waste perfectly good teaching materials. So, I approached my teachers and asked them for the papers. I was obliged, and my little seven, eight and nine-year old face simply shined with happiness as if I had won the California State Lottery!

When I would arrive home with all the papers, my mother was shocked, but she allowed me to keep them. I was always grateful to her for that. Many other mothers would have told their children to throw the papers out. By allowing me to keep the materials, my mother was helping me to develop into the educator I am today. Was this not excellent foresight on the part of my mother? Of course, it was. She saw what was budding in me.

My mother was very encouraging. She always believed in my dreams. She never told me I could not do something. Instead, she encouraged me. And, instead of telling me who I should be in life or what career I should have, she asked me what I wanted to do. Once I told her, my words became her words. After telling her once when I was eight years old I would become a teacher, she told everyone from that point forward I would become a teacher. She knew me well enough to know that I was not a wishy-washy person and I said what I meant (even as a child).

During the summer months, when my brothers and I would be home and when my cousins would come over for summer break, I would teach class to them with use of all the worksheets I had collected. I was their teacher, and they were my students. They may not have liked it too much, but they obliged me. I am grateful to them for allowing me to practice on them.

When I was a teenager, my mother and I began to have a rocky relationship. I no longer wanted to live in her home. I constantly daydreamed of running away to my grandmother's home. At the time, I did not know that subconsciously I blamed her for the abuse I suffered from men who committed underhanded devilment upon me, from age three to eleven. I figured as my protector, my parent, the chief guard on the post, she should have known all that transpired. I, however, did not run away. I endured until I was eighteen, and then, I ran off to college.

The actions of these other people caused a wedge between my mother and me. Although I loved my mother dearly, I blamed her for being blind. It wasn't until my adult years that I came to the realization that she had no knowledge of the transgressions that were committed against me. Once I came into this realization, I spent the rest of her life letting her know I loved her and did not blame her for what she had not known.

What was worse was the fact she did not know until I was in my late twenties why I had pulled away from her. I always expected her to know, and she always expected me to tell her. But, we had never developed a relationship of communication. My mother was very quiet. She didn't say much. As she watched me, she saw me as a bright child, and with that, she thought I knew more than I did and that I would automatically tell her certain things. When I did something wrong, she would say, "I never expected you to do that, Cassundra." I would be utterly shocked that I had severely disappointed her, and I would be totally confounded that she expected me to know more than she had taught me. I was only a young child. But, her comments made me think and do better than I was doing.

After graduating high school and going to college, I later decided to get married. My mother was very excited. She held onto the tradition of the bride's family paying for the wedding, even though she was once again a divorced mother with my youngest brother yet to raise. He is seven years younger than I am. So, he was fourteen at the time.

My mother made all the wedding arrangements. She bought my wedding dress, the invitations, all the food, etc. I know this was an awesome task. But, she never complained. She was happy to do it. Even when my fiancé's parents offered to help, she refused. I am her daughter, and she was footing the bill.

Before the delivery of my first son, when I began having contractions, my mother rode the bus to my home because she did not have a car. She stayed with me all day. She even took me for a walk in the park to move the birthing process along. When I gave birth to both of my two sons (two years and seven months apart), Aaron Michael White and Daron Christopher White, my mother was in the delivery room with me, along with their father, my then-husband.

As my life went on, my mother continued to be there to support mostly everything I did- not the dumb stuff. When I needed advice about my children, she was there to listen first and then instruct. When I needed to vent about something, she was there to listen. When I decided to write my first book, she was very excited with me. When I decided to purchase a home, she supported my decision. When I asked her to assist in the pre-sale of my fifth book, she presold over 50 copies. My mother was a great trooper. I called her my number one cheerleader. Every event I hosted, she came- unless she absolutely could not make it, which was rare. When I formed my ministry- International Women's Commission, she was the Chief Financial Officer.

My mother was simply wonderful, sweet, and kind. She did not say a lot, but when she did, she meant to be heard. As a child, I feared my mother because I knew she meant business. She was not the one to have the wool pulled over her eyes. As an adult, I had the utmost respect for her. I admired her tenacity and her faithfulness. I admired her unending source of love for her family, especially her children and grandchildren.

After she completed the task of raising her four children (my three brothers and me), she was able to live her life as a single woman who was yet a mother and a grandmother. At age forty-one, she had fulfilled her motherly obligations, and she was free! Mothers all love that time in their lives. It is a time that is anticipated. It does not mean they love their children any less, but they have faithfully seen them to adulthood, a point where they can be responsible for themselves. This is another characteristic I loved about my mother. She allowed her children to be independent. She did not hover over us as though we were yet little children. She allowed us to go and make our own choices, whether good or bad. With my independent spirit, this worked well for our relationship.

At approximately fifty-two years of age, my mother began to experience problems with her heart. As time went on, she would experience blockage of her heart arteries, which caused her to need a stint to open one of the arteries. She was told to change her diet and other life patterns/habits. However, after living any lifestyle for an extended period of time, change is hard to accomplish. Having successes and failures with making the doctor's requested changes, my mother's health conditions worsened.

On March 7, 2010, my mother departed this life as a result of arteriosclerosis (hardening of the arteries). Her heart had been overworking itself to pump blood throughout her body. Eventually, her heart simply stopped, and she went to meet her maker.

At the time of her death, at age 57, my mother was yet a mother of four children as well as a grandmother of eight. Her grandchildren, at the time of her passing, ranged in ages from 11-23. She had become a grandmother at the age of thirty-four. Also, she had one great-grandson, who was approximately two years old at the time of her passing. Today, she has four great grandchildren and one on the way.

My mother was always a source of great inspiration to me. I saw her climb the ladder of success at her place of employment where she began as a bus driver. One month after securing her position, she began working in the accounting department of the same company. For a short time, she drove the bus and did accounting. After some time, it was requested that she leave bus driving and simply do accounting. Before long, she became the accounting manager. She did all of this with natural skill, ability, and determination, for she did not graduate high school nor did she have a degree.

With all my mother did, she left a legacy of LOVE. She taught my brothers and me to stand together, for we are family. She did not say this with words. Instead, she demonstrated it, and we follow suit.

What I am most grateful for is the belief my mother instilled in me- "I can do all things through Christ who strengthens me." She taught me to have unconditional confidence in myself, and to this day, it exudes from every essence of my being. She taught me to always be strong. With her as my example, I am, and I will continue to be as I stand on the Word of my Rock- Jesus the Christ, who is my Lord and my Savior. In Him I live, I move and I have my being.

The love my brothers (Noah, Rod, and August) and I have for our mother, along with the love our children have for her, is a love that is strong, a love that is never ending, and a love that will endure all. Why? Because her love is *undying*!

Momma, Ma, Punkin- from all your children (4), grandchildren (8), and great-grandchildren (5)- we love you today and forever more!

A Mother's Love Shines, even during the Darkest of Times

The Dr. Cassundra White-Elliott Story
by
Daron C. White

A Mother's Heart

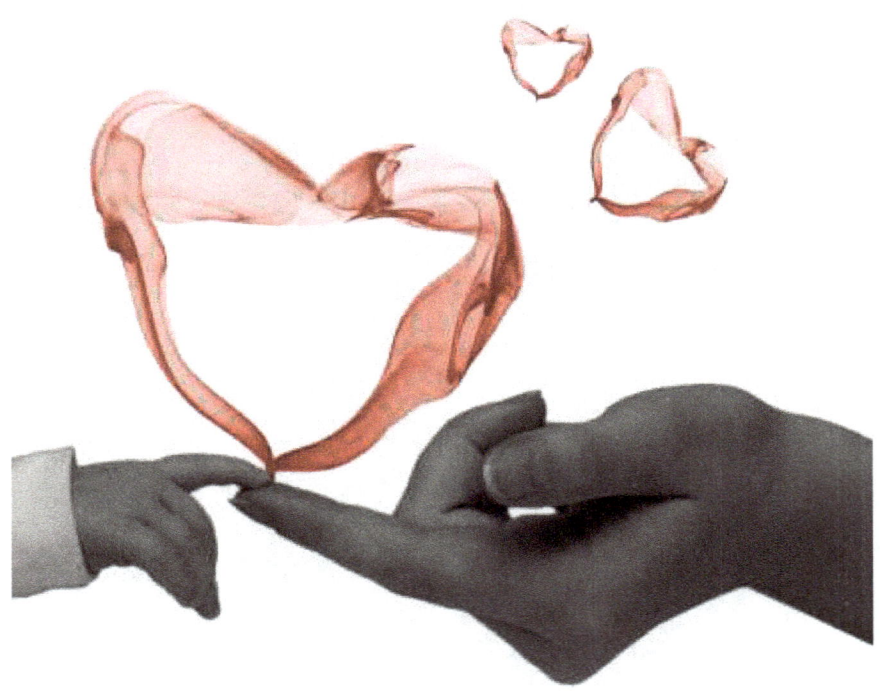

A Mother's Heart

We all have a person that we can say is the reason that we are the person that we are today. That person for me is and has always has been my mother. My mother worked extremely hard to create a comfortable life for me and my brother. She has supported us with everything that we have done, and she has been there to help get us on the right path when we stepped off onto a dark path. My mom always motivated me to be all that I can be and supports me in everything.

With sports, my mom was always my biggest supporter. When I was a child, she would come out to practices and all of my games. She never let work stop her from cheering me on; she may have been late, or had to leave early, but she was still there in the stands to cheer me on. During my high school years, my mother would come out to every home game and close away games if she could. She was more than just a fan; she was my motivation. To some, this may seem like nothing, but to me, it meant everything.

My mom wasn't just there for me in sports, but in my education. Whenever I needed help with school, no matter the subject, she was there to help me- even today. When I got kicked out of school, she became my teacher, so that I could stay on track. She is the reason that I am not only studying to get my Bachelor's degree, but also my Master's degree. Since I was a young boy, my mother has always stressed the importance of education, and I am thankful for it.

The main thing that my mother stressed the importance of is having a relationship with God. My mom took my brother Aaron and me back to church when I was six and has been a strong member of the church since then. My mother got involved in church from the start. She started out teaching children's church. Since I was a child, she taught me about God first hand. And after her children's church days, she stayed involved in the church and made sure that my brother and I stayed involved in the church as well, and she found ways for us participate in the youth programs. There was a time that we would attend Sunday school, morning church service and the evening service. My mom stopped taking us trick or treating and started taking us to the church Harvest Festival celebration. My mom made sure that we knew that Jesus was the reason for every season.

I felt my mom's love the most when my father's presence was unstable in my life. My father was in and out of my life for a long time until he finally stopped picking me and my brother up every other weekend for a couple of years. My father wasn't completely out of my life, but he may as well have been. I would only speak to him every couple of months, and every time he would make promises that he never kept. I would always remember him telling me that he would pick me up for the weekend, and I would pack my bag and wait all day and night for him just be let down. The pain that I felt could only be replaced by one thing.

The one thing that could help me get over the pain of my father's absence was my mother's love. Every time my father broke a promise, my mom was right there to put the pieces back together. When my father promised to take my brother and me fishing and did not, my mother asked my grandmother to take us. When my father wasn't there to teach me how to throw a football, my mother asked one of my uncles to do it. When I needed to learn how to tie a tie when I was in private school, my mother had someone teach her, and she taught me. Later in life, when I had forgotten how to tie a tie, my mother asked her godfather to teach me. When my brother and I needed male role models, she made us become ushers at our church, so we could be surrounded by God-fearing men. If there was something that my mom couldn't do for us or if she was unable to teach us something, she would find someone that could.

The things that my mother could do for me and my brother, she did. She taught us how to ride our bikes, tie our shoes, brush our teeth, do our own laundry, and how to pray. She took us on family vacations, so we could experience new things and see the world. She wanted us be like the other kids and play sports, so she enrolled us in every sport until we were old enough to decide which sports we wanted to play. My mother taught me how to be a God-fearing and trusting man.

My mother is more than just the average mother; she has put on many hats and played many roles in my life. She has been both my mother and my father, and I thank her for being that to me. I'm proud and honored to call Dr. Cassundra White-Elliott my mother.

Gift of Salvation for Non-Believers

"For all have sinned, and come short of the glory of God."
Romans 3:23

This section was written especially for non-believers, those who have not accepted the gift of salvation. The gift of salvation saves souls from eternal damnation and is a free gift offered by God himself. John 3:16-18 says, *"For God so loved the world, that he gave his only begotten Son, that whosoever believeth in him should not perish, but have everlasting life. For God sent not his Son into the world to condemn the world; but that the world through him might be saved. He that believeth on him is not condemned: but he that believeth not is condemned already, because he hath not believed in the name of the only begotten Son of God."* This section of scripture tells us God's purpose for giving His son Jesus to the world. The world was in a bad condition. The world was overwrought with sin; the people were living for fleshly desires rather than for God's desires.

As a result of the world's conditions, God decided that He would offer the perfect sacrifice that would save the world from being a place where people were lost and had no hope. He decided that His own son could stand in proxy for the sin-filled world, taking all sin upon Himself.

So Jesus came, born of a virgin, to save this dying world. He walked on this earth for 33 ½ years, doing the work of His Heavenly Father. At the appointed time, He died by way of crucifixion upon a cross at Calvary, on Golgatha's hill. He shed his blood and died for you and for me. Because His blood was pure, it paid the penalty for all unrighteousness and gave those who believe in Him direct access to His father's throne.

Scripture tells us in Matthew 27:51 that the veil of the temple was ripped in two from top to bottom, at the moment that Jesus' spirit left His body. As a result of the veil's removal, we are no longer required to have a high priest make intercession for us. We, as the children of the Most High God, are able to approach the throne God for ourselves, and Jesus sits on the right hand of the Father making intercession for us.

But what is even more miraculous than God offering His own son as the perfect sacrifice was the fact that when Jesus was placed in grave clothes and placed in a tomb, He only remained there until the third day. God would not have it that His son would remain in the heart of the earth forever. In order for people to believe in the awesome power of God and His dear son Jesus, a miracle had to be performed. So, on the third day, after Jesus died on the cross, He was resurrected, demonstrating the omnipotence of God. This very act was the act that would cause people to believe in a god that reigns supreme and holds the power of the universe in His very hands, a god that could save them from themselves.

Today, if you are an unbeliever, you can change your destiny. You can change where you will spend your eternity. Our Heavenly Father gives us the freedom of choice about how we want to live our life here on earth and how we want to spend eternity. In Deuteronomy 30:19, God boldly declares, *"I call heaven and earth to record this day against you, that I have set before you life and death, blessing and cursing: therefore choose life, that both thou and thy seed may live."*

So, dear friend what choice will you make today? Will you spend your eternity with the Creator or will you suffer Hell's eternal flames? Again, the choice is yours. Just as the men aboard the ship who were with Jonah became believers, you too can make a choice to accept the only one and true living God as your god.

If after reading the above passages, you have decided that you want to spend your eternity in Heaven with God, the creator, and His son Jesus, and the Holy Spirit, read through what has affectionately come to be known as the Roman's Road. This is the road to salvation. As you read through the scriptures that comprise the Roman's Road, you will also read the explanation for each scripture so you will have clarity about what you are reading and confessing.

The Roman's Road to Salvation

The road to salvation begins with Romans 3:23 which declares, *"For all have sinned, and come short of the glory of God."* This scripture explains that everyone has come short of God's glory and needs redemption. Then Romans 6:23a states, *"For the wages of sin is death."* Here, we learn that the consequence of living a life of sin is death. Everyone will experience physical death as a result of the sin committed in the garden of Eden, but those who commit themselves to a life of sin will suffer eternal damnation in the lake of fire (Rev. 19).

Continue with the rest of verse 6:23 that says, *"but the gift of God is eternal life through Jesus Christ our Lord."* There is an alternative to suffering eternal damnation. We can accept the gift of salvation by accepting Jesus as our personal lord and savior. Then, Romans 5:8 says, *"But God commendeth his love toward us, in that, while we were yet sinners, Christ died for us."* We are able to receive the gift of salvation because Christ came to earth and shed His blood for us on the cross.

Continue to Romans 10: 9-10 which says, *"That if thou shalt confess with thy mouth the Lord Jesus, and shalt believe in thine heart that God hath raised him from the dead, thou shalt be saved. For with the heart man believeth unto righteousness; and with the mouth confession is made unto salvation.*" If we confess with our mouths that Jesus is the son of God, that he came and died for our sins, and that God raised Him from the dead, we will receive salvation.

Finish with Romans 10:13, which states, "*For whosoever shall call upon the name of the Lord shall be saved.*" Call upon the name of God by saying these words, "**Lord Jesus, come into my heart and save me Lord. I believe that you are the Son of God who came and died on the cross for my sins. I believe that you rose from the grave. I also believe that you now sit in heaven on the right side of the Father, making intersession for me. I accept you as my Lord and my Savior.**"

Now that you have confessed with your mouth that Jesus is the son of God and that He died for our sins and rose from the grave, **YOU ARE NOW SAVED!!!!** You will spend your eternity in heaven.

The next step is very important- you must find a bible-based church that teaches the word of God and confesses the Lord Jesus Christ to be the son of God. Don't delay. Do this immediately. Do not leave yourself open to the enemy. Get connected with the saints of the Most High God and keep yourself covered with the unspotted blood of the lamb.

Here is my prayer for you.

Father God,

I thank you for the opportunity to minister your word to the unsaved, the unchurched, and the uncommitted. Father God, I pray now for the souls who have just received the gift of salvation. Lord Father, they have opened their hearts to you, and I know that you have received them into your kingdom and written their names in the Book of Life. Father God, I pray that you will touch their lives and show yourself mightily before them. Let their eyes be opened by the scales falling off, allowing them to see clearly.

Father God, I even pray for the backslider, those who have turned away from you after receiving the gift of salvation. You said in your word that you desire that none would perish. So Lord, I send your word to them right now praying that they would confess the iniquity in their heart, repent, and turn from their evil ways, so that they may receive a life of abundance. You said in your word in Matthew Chapter 14, that every knee shall bow before you and every tongue will confess that Jesus is Lord.

Father God, I pray now that we all come under subjection to your word and that we will humbly submit our lives to you. I ask all these things in the name of my Lord and Savior Jesus Christ. Amen, Amen, Amen!!!!

I will continue to pray for your success in your walk with God. Remember, this spiritual walk that you are about to embark on will not be an easy walk, but remember, the race is not given to the swift but to those who endure to the end.

Be blessed with heaven's best. I love you!

A Mother's Heart

ABOUT THE EDITOR

Dr. Cassundra White-Elliott resides in California with her family, where as an English/Education professor she works for various community colleges and universities. One of the universities she teaches for is the Southern California Branch of the University of Phoenix. There she teaches communication studies.

When writing, she writes with the direction of the Holy Spirit, in an effort to share with God's people all that He has for them.

In addition to teaching and writing, Dr. White-Elliott also serves as an evangelistic teacher. She is also the founder of International Women's Commission, a ministry that serves the needs of the entire person, by attending to healing the mind, body, soul, and spirit.

Dr. White-Elliott holds a Ph.D. in Education, a Master's in English Composition, and a Bachelor's in Education.

Dr. White-Elliott is also the founder of CLF Publishing, LLC. For your publishing needs, go online to www.clfpublishing.org.

A Mother's Heart

OTHER BOOKS BY THE EDITOR

(All books can be purchased at www.creativemindsbookstore)

A Mother's Heart

From Despair, through Determination, to Victory!

A lot can happen during a span of 40 years. The life of Dr. Cassundra White-Elliott has been anything but uneventful. From a fun-loving childhood sprinkled with incidents of abuse to a tumultuous young adulthood to a stable, secure adult life, she has experienced a full life, with much more to come. Her story is inspiring and motivating.

If anyone lacks hope, reading Dr. White-Elliott's autobiography will propel him/her into an attitude of "Maybe I can." This attitude, if nurtured and developed, will grow into an attitude of "Yes, I can." Throughout her life, Cassundra has always held in her heart the belief that she could achieve anything that she had a made-up mind to embark upon. She was determined to achieve her heart's desires, doing what God has called her to do. She takes no credit for herself. All the glory goes to God, for He is her driving force. In Him, she lives, moves, and has her being.

Through the Storm

Preview

Through the Storm was duly inspired by the avaricious cloud of depression that decided to hover overhead of my daily existence in the latter part of 2007. Although I found it extremely difficult, I was once again compelled to not be defeated by just another snare that the enemy, the trickster, set for me. Once again, or more appropriately I should say *continuously*, he has exerted pernicious efforts to snatch the very life out of me by causing me to wallow in despair and to believe that I had been overcome by failure when in actuality and all reality, I was just experiencing a temporary set back. During those cloudy days, I had to remind myself daily that even though I was a target of the enemy, I am and will always be a child of the Most High god, Jehovah, who is my rock, my stability.

In my last book **Dare to Succeed by Breaking through Barriers**, I discuss many barriers people find themselves faced with and the keys to successfully breaking through and overcoming those barriers. However, upon the release of the book, I too found myself faced with barriers, barriers in their multiplicitous form. Just as I reminded my readers, I had to continuously remind myself that one of the benefits of being God's child is the ability to be victorious in all battles, which comes from standing firm and continuing to fight the good fight of faith believing that I am an over comer and a conqueror as told to me in Romans 8:37.

During the midst of these seemingly perilous times, a dear friend gave me a cd by the Williams Brothers. While driving and listening, tears streamed from my eyes as I listened to the words of one particular song, "Still Here." The song says,

Heartaches, I've had my shares of heartaches, but I'm still here
Trouble, I've seen my share of troubles, but I'm still here
Bruises, I've taken my lumps & bruises, I but I'm still here
Loneliness, I've had my share of loneliness, but I'm still here

Through it all I've made it through another day's journey, God kept me here
I've made it through another days journey, God kept me here
Lied on, many times I've been lied on, but I'm still here
Burdens, I had to bare so many burdens, but I'm still here
Dark days, I've had my share of dark days, but I'm still here
Disappointments, I've had so many disappointments, but I'm still here

Chorus
It's by the grace of God, that I'm still here today
He was always there, no matter what came my way
I felt the presence of him, in my time of need
Standing right there, just to seal my faith

Chorus
I made it (I made it)
I made it (yes, I made it)
I'm still here (I'm still here)
A lot of folks say that I wouldn't be here tonight, but I made it (I

made it)
By the grace of God, yall (yes, I made it)
I'm still here (I'm still here)

I have to lay awake in the midnight hour sometimes, tossing & turning (I made it)
All night long (yes, I made)
Have anyone had to lay awake all night long sometime (I'm still here)
Tears in your eyes wandering what the next day was gonna bring (I made it)
God kept has arms around you, yes he did (yes, I made it)
You made through the trails (I'm still here)

Come on let me see those hands in the air
I made it, I made it (I made it)
I made it, I made it (yes, I made it)
I made it, I made it (I'm still here)
Through it all (through it all I'm still hereeee)

To me, every word uttered in this song exemplified both my past and present experiences. But the triumph in it all was the victory that was in my grasp. I knew that I had to praise my way through to a new season.

But before victory was attained, with all the burdens that weighed heavily upon me, day after day I seemed to sink further and further, deeper and deeper into an abyss of depression. I fervently tried to shake it. But to avoid the daily pressures, that my life was consumed with, I would sleep later and later each day, in an attempt to avoid the world at large, which seemed to want to swallow me whole. This continued to the point where I would even turn the phone off to avoid not only the insolent bill collectors but also loved ones. I didn't avoid loved ones because I didn't love them any longer. No, I avoided them because I did not want them to hear in my voice the anguish I was enduring.

The irony of it all, though, was that I believed the word of God, and I knew unequivocally that He had not forgotten me and that he would not forsake me, for He had given me a life of blessings and he had already shown me glimpses of a very bright and promising future.

Unleashed Anger, Anger Unleashed

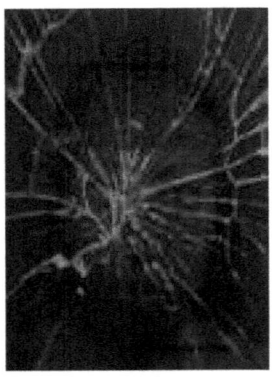

Preview

Introduction
What Is This Book All About?

As I prepared to embark upon the adventure of writing this book, I had to prepare myself to also be transparent. I have found that being transparent is required in order for healing to transpire, healing for all those that peruse the pages of this book and myself. And I may as well tell you that today, at the onset of this project, I have not been totally delivered from my condition of being an anger-filled person. However, I am definitely a work in progress. I have made strides with the assistance of my Lord and Savior, Jesus Christ, who is the head of my life. Without his love, guidance, and teachings, I would not be the woman of God I am today. I shudder to think where I could be instead and will therefore not entertain the thought.

Rather, I will confess that it is my desire that a transformation will result as I do an in-depth exploration of who I started out as when I was a little girl, the woman I became, and the woman that I am striving to be. It is my endeavor to see God tear down walls that encapsulate both my mind and soul and free me from the bondages of anger. It is my prayer that total deliverance will come between the writing of this sentence and the very last one of the book.

So, it is at this point that I must stop and utter a word of prayer.

Oh Heavenly Father,
I just want to stop and take another moment to give you praise, honor, and glory for being just who you are. You are the Alpha and the Omega. You are the finisher of my faith, for you knew my beginning before I departed from my mother's womb and you know my ending as well. Father God, I just want to thank you for your grace, the grace that you have afforded me, oh Lord, to still be here and to be able to tell my story. A story that will set captives free, present company included. Father God, I just want to tell you that I love you because you love me in spite of me. You love me with all my imperfections. You love me because as it says in your word that I am a royal priesthood. I am the daughter of the Most High God; I am the daughter of the King of Kings. Father God, I thank you for your love and the strength to be able to cause this work to come to manifestation. Oh Lord Father, I humble in your sight. I place my face to the ground and cry out your name. I cry out for healing in the name of my Lord and Savior, Jesus Christ. I believe that you will give me favor and grace to heal and to let your glory reign mightily in my life. So, therefore I place my life back into your hands, so that you can do a mighty work. I enter this prayer in the name of your son, Jesus Christ.
Amen.

Readers, as the writing of this book takes me through my transformation, I pray that the reading and re-reading of it will take you through yours. If you desire to be free, as I do, remember freedom can be yours. It is a gift for believers of the Almighty God. We just need to first believe that we can be free, pray for freedom, receive our freedom (by the necessary path as revealed to us by the Holy Spirit), and then confess with our mouths that we are free and are no longer bound.

Dare to Succeed by Breaking through Barriers

Preview

Introduction

Over the past few years, while conversing with family, friends, associates, strangers and even my students, I have noticed a common pattern amongst believers and non-believers alike. In both groups, there are those who make things happen because of the belief system they live by, and there are others who tend to demonstrate debilitating thoughts about the very course of their lives. Those who demonstrate debilitating thoughts do not seem to believe that their destiny is controllable. They tend to believe that whatever is supposed to happen will happen- on its own. As a result of this type of thinking, they don't put much effort into the outcome of their future, or should I say not as much effort as they could. For non-believers, this attitude and behavior is understandable because some non-believers are driven by their own self will while others have a lack of self will and are, therefore, not driven at all. But for believers who have the word of God, as a guide for their lives, I call this attitude living a substandard life compared to the one that God planned for His children. This is a result of failing to tap into the inheritance that God himself promised believers in His holy word.

Living a substandard life simply means living below one's capabilities. Many people believe that it is the set of talents each of us has been gifted with that enables us to be productive and live a prosperous life. Although our talents and how we use them have much to do with our earthly success and will lend to our prosperity, for believers our talents are not our only resources. God is our source for prosperity and He dispenses it to us. That is not to say that there are not varying levels of prosperity because there are and just like grace it is not dispensed by God evenly amongst men.

However, there are many believers who have failed to tap into the very essence of their beings. They are not tapping into their God-given talents nor are they using the power of prayer to tap into the prosperity that God desires for His children. The bible tells us that, *"the effectual fervent prayer of a righteous man availeth much"* (James 5:16b). When people live below their capabilities, they are not doing everything within their power to live a prosperous and fulfilled life. In many cases, there is one explanation for why we live below our means. Outside of the reasons of just not caring or being unaware of the word of God, in many cases there are barriers that stem from the past that block prosperity and prevent us from moving ahead into the future that God has designed for us.

For non-believers, whatever is in their physical, mental, financial, and educational power is what patterns their lives. Believers, on the other hand, have all these resources available to them with one added bonus. They have the power of the Holy Spirit available to them.

Public Speaking in the Spiritual Arena

Preview

Chapter Two
How Communication Works

Purpose: This chapter will explain the six primary components of communication, identifying their purpose and how they work together.

The Source

In oral communication, the source of information is the speaker. In a church setting, the foundation of the message is God's word, but it is a speaker's interpretation of God's word that is delivered to the audience. As speakers vary, the information may vary but should have a similar essence because the foundational text is the same.

The Message

The message is the collective set of ideas that the speaker (the source) wants to deliver and/or illustrate to the audience. The message can be informative where the speaker informs the audience about a specific set of information. Or, the message may be persuasive in nature if the speaker wants to persuade the audience about conducting themselves in a specific manner, accepting God's commandments, or any number of things.

The Audience
The audience is the person or persons who are to receive the message. In the spiritual arena, there are many instances where an audience is present. It may be a traditional worship service, bible study, a conference, or a meeting. In any case, those who are there to receive the message from the audience, regardless of the number of individuals.

Where is Your Joppa?

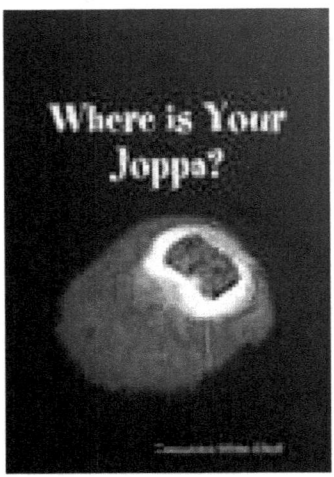

Introduction

Where is Your Joppa? was written for the express purpose of illustrating God's call for obedience in the lives of believers with respect to the individual call that He has on each of our lives. As you read throughout the various chapters, notice that the emphasis is placed on our persistent disobedience in answering God's call in a specific area of our lives. We have become a people who are similar to the Israelites when they found themselves in the middle of the wilderness, following their exodus from Egypt. Before God, they murmured and complained about their current life conditions and failed to be obedient to God's statutes delivered through His servant Moses. Their persistent disobedience caused them to lose the opportunity to see and enter the Promised Land. I ask you, "What has your disobedience cost you?" "Was your disobedience worth what it cost you?" "Do you think about the souls you could have ushered into the kingdom of God?" These are some of the questions that I pray will be answered through your reading of the book.

The first chapter following this introduction provides a detailed interpretation and analysis of the Book of Jonah, which serves as the foundational text for this book. Jonah, a prophet of God, commits an act of disobedience out of a spirit of pride and superiority. We, like Jonah, may also be afflicted with a spirit that prevents us from being obedient to God's call. Some of us are afflicted with pride, bitterness, unforgiveness, and rebellion, to name a few. These spirits are direct impediments to our obedience. However, others may not be afflicted with a spirit at all. We may be operating out of ignorance, not knowing that what we *are* doing is preventing us from what we *should* be doing.

Following the exegesis, the next three chapters (2-4) will provide examples of people today who walk in a spirit of disobedience. Using the theme "Joppa," I will pinpoint various situations that have occurred in the lives of several individuals that served as impediments to answering God-given mandates. What you may find surprising is that particular situations, relationships, or tasks that we may deem as honorable may indeed be impediments *if* we have allowed them to become a means of escape from what God has called us to do. So the situations themselves are not negative, but when we allow them to supersede God's call, our actions become negative. Reading these scenarios will prepare you for chapter five.

Chapter 5 discusses the necessity to perform a self evaluation. In order to see whether or not our lives indeed need to be turned around, we must be honest with ourselves about whether or not we have run from the call of God and situated ourselves in a safe haven, our very own "Joppa." When we honestly examine ourselves and allow the Holy Spirit to show us what lies deep within the recesses of our hearts, we provide ourselves with an opportunity to get our lives in order. Whether or not we actually make a change is something all together different.

After doing an honest assessment of our spiritual walk with God and unveiling any hidden "Joppas," we have to determine the right time to walk in obedience. Everyone has his/her own season for doing what God has mandated. Some of our seasons are right now, and some of our seasons are in a time to come. Knowing the right time to move is just as important as answering God's call. Therefore, Chapter 6 will discuss God's timing for us to move and for us to be still.

Finally, during the writing of this book, the Holy Spirit led me to appeal to the unbeliever. Chapter 7 is directed to the unbeliever, providing an opportunity for salvation.

As you read through the various chapters of the book, I pray that you will be receptive to the written words on the pages that were written under the direction of the Holy Spirit, as well as the words the Holy Spirit will undoubtedly speak directly to you about your own situation. Finally, do not hesitate to share this book with those whom the Holy Spirit leads you to.

I pray that the spirit of fear will not entrap you.

I pray that you will yield yourself as a willing vessel to our Heavenly Father.

I pray that you will answer the call that God has on your life.

Remember, I Samuel 15:22b states, "To obey is better than sacrifice."

Mayhem in the Hamptons

Romero and Yolanda optimistically plan for the day that is going to change their lives from being single persons to a couple who is united in holy matrimony. They, along with their parents, close friends and family, fly over to the infamous Hamptons, where only the rich and famous vacation, to have their dream wedding at the five-star Hampton Suites located on a peninsula in the Hamptons. Little do they know that their perfect day will turn out to be less than perfect when their wedding planner Mariesha Coleman suddenly goes missing!

A time when the newlyweds' lives should be filled with joy and the creation of wonderful memories, they are stricken with grief as they desperately try to find clues to help solve Mariesha's disappearance.

Mayhem in the Hamptons is a tale that shares how the horrors of a woman's past can come back to haunt her in more than one way and the impact it can have on anyone who gets in the way.

Preacher's Daughter

Tinisha, the daughter of a preacher, is a twenty-six year old God-fearing young woman endeavoring to complete law school so that she can make her mark in the courtroom.

Working in one of the late-night clubs in Hollywood to earn money to pay her own way through school, Tinisha soon learns that life doesn't always go as planned. Finding her strength in her faith, Tinisha constantly finds herself praying as she watches God move miraculously in her life.

Preacher's Son

Romero Turner is a private investigator with a promising future. As he continues to build his career, he is excited about the cases he undertakes. However, his father Pastor Theodore Turner has other plans for his son's life. In the midst of trying to save his client's husband from Sylvestor Domingo, a ruthless crime lord, Romero must try to salvage his relationship with his father. He must decide if ministry or life as a detective is in his future.

Lord, Teach Me to be a Blessing!

Lord, Teach Me to be a Blessing! will change a person's mentality from being centered around "me, myself, and I" to focusing on "others."

The world system teaches us that it is acceptable to place ourselves above others in an attempt to get ahead and even to survive. Herbert Spencer coined the phrase '*survival of the fittest*' after reading Charles Darwin's theory of evolution. This concept of surpassing and outdoing others is the world's philosophy.

However, the word of God does not subscribe to or promote this self-centered ideology, and therefore, neither should believers. We must hold fast to the truths outlined in Holy Scripture: "*Love thy neighbor as you love thyself*" (James 2:8) and "*It is more blessed to give than to receive*" (Acts 20:35).

While holding God's truths to be self evident, we must demonstrate them to others, thereby showing them the way of the Lord of how to be a blessing to someone *rather* than looking to receive a blessing.

This is the very purpose of this book: to change the mentality of the world from being *self* centered to *other* centered.

After the Dust Settles

Throughout the journey of life, we all experience ups and downs and joys and pains. Most of us successfully find solutions to the situations/problems we encounter, but we often avoid dealing with the attached emotions. If we continue to ignore the emotions of pain, hurt, disappointment, anger, etc., we set ourselves up for destruction. Our families, our cultures, and our society tell us to be strong, to keep our chin up, and to grin and bear it. However, these methods of avoidance can lead us to strokes due to the undue amount of pressure we place on ourselves and/or mental illness from being unable to cope with the emotional baggage we have accumulated.

In *After the Dust Settles,* Dr. C. White-Elliott shares several situations that we all may encounter at one time or another in our lifetime and how to successfully navigate through them, so we can find ourselves emotionally healthy after the dust has settled and the situation has been rectified.

Begin reading today and experience a better tomorrow!

www.ingramcontent.com/pod-product-compliance
Lightning Source LLC
Chambersburg PA
CBHW070738160426
43192CB00009B/1489